RECORDED VERSIONS GUITAR

AUTHENTIC TRANSCRIPTIONS
WITH NOTES AND TABLATURE

PAT MET
TRIO → LIVE

Music transcriptions by Alejandro Moro

ISBN 0-634-04643-8

HAL•LEONARD®
CORPORATION

7777 W. BLUEMOUND RD. P.O. BOX 13819 MILWAUKEE, WI 53213

Visit Hal Leonard Online at
www.halleonard.com

CONTENTS

Bright Size Life

By Pat Metheny

*Chord symbols reflect implied harmony.

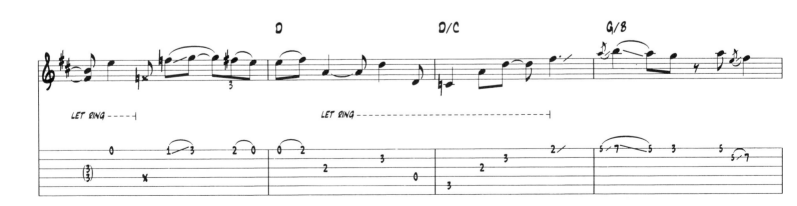

*PLAYED BEHIND THE BEAT.

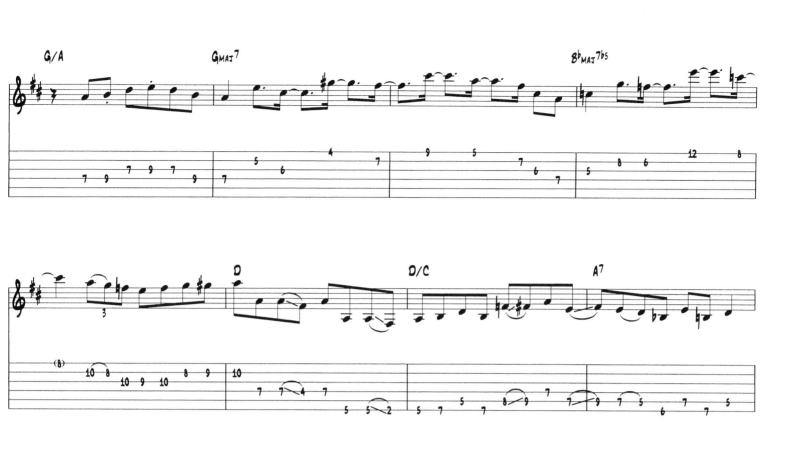

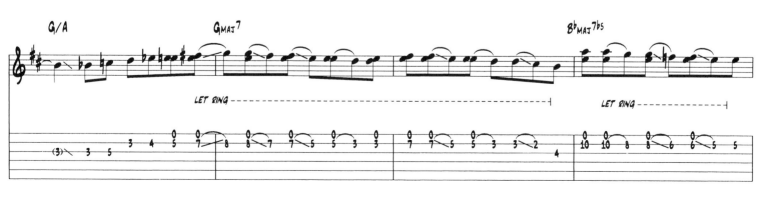

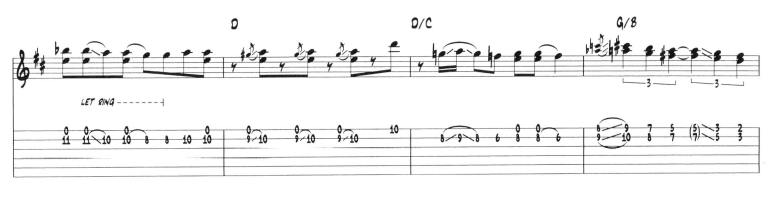

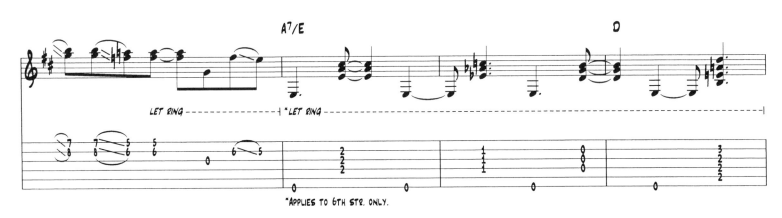

*Applies to 6th str. only.

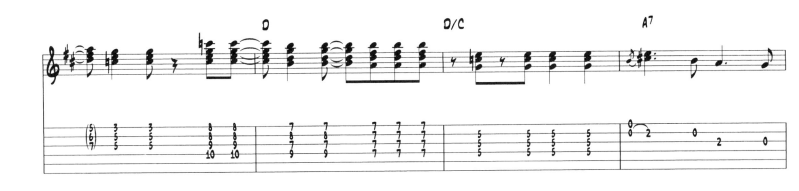

8

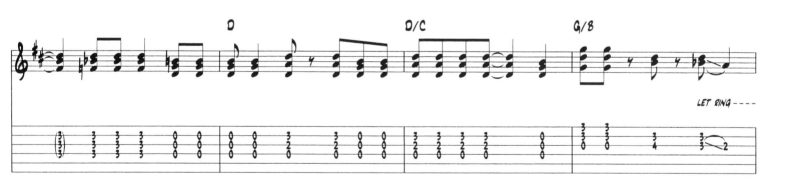

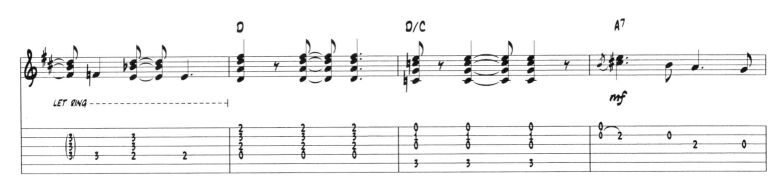

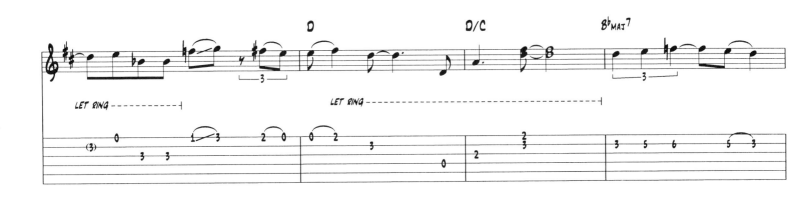

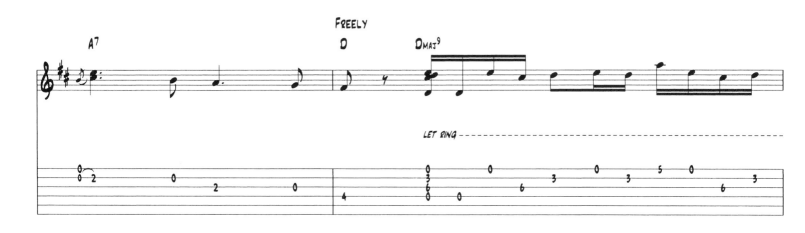

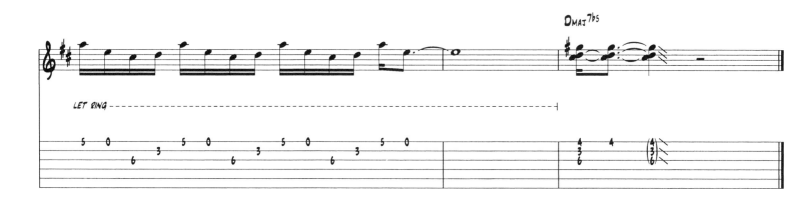

Question & Answer

By Pat Metheny

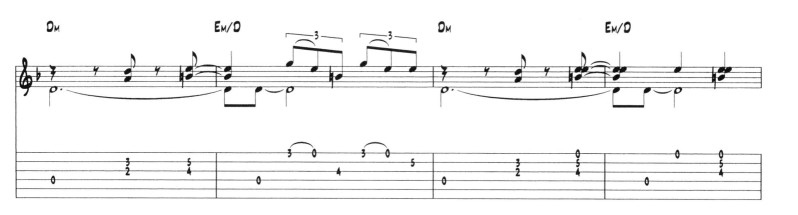

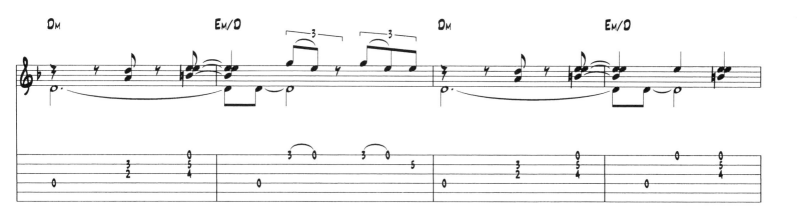

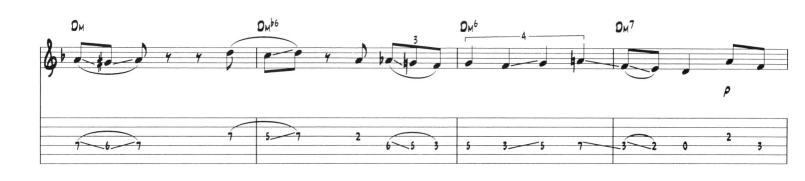

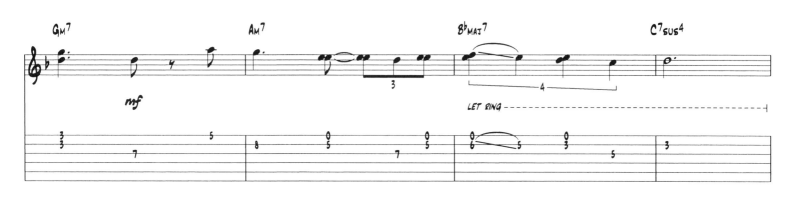

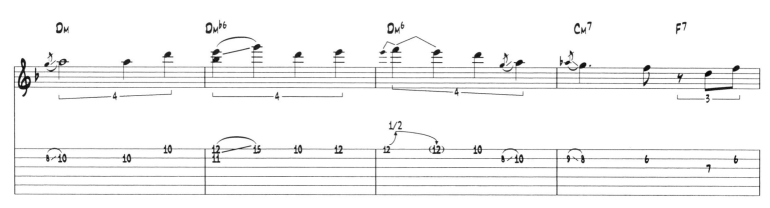

*Played behind the beat.

18

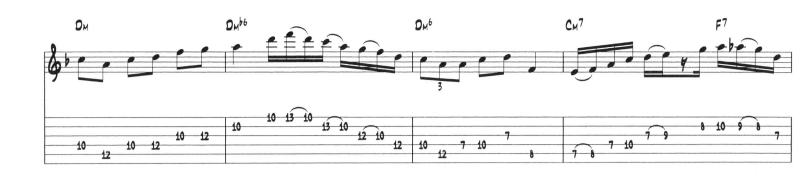

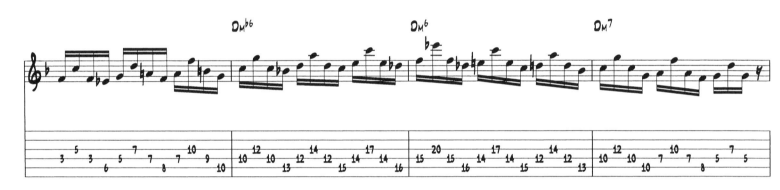
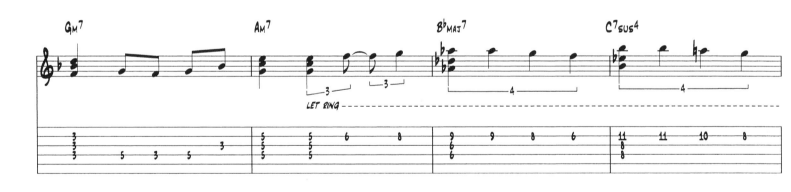
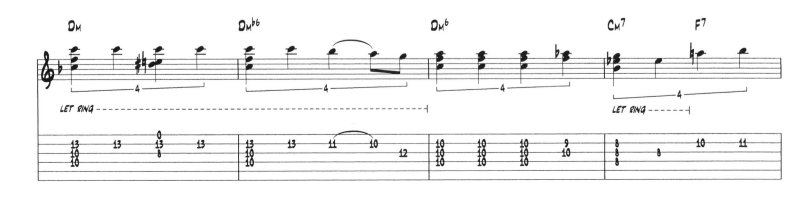

20

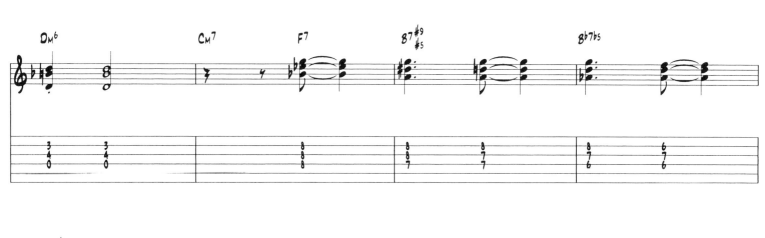

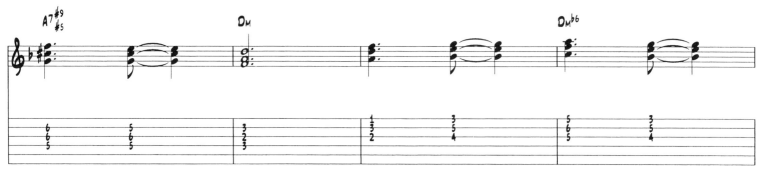

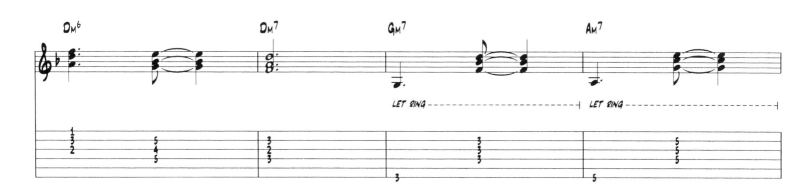

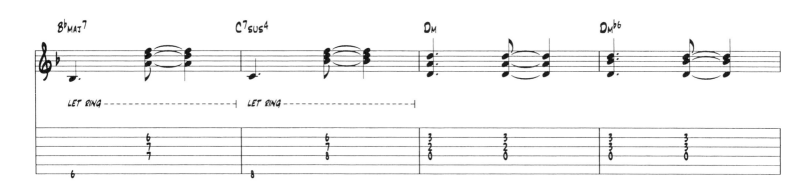

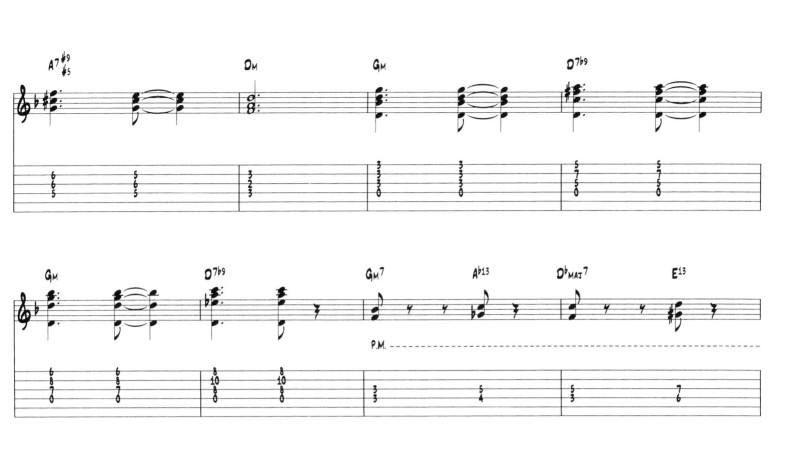

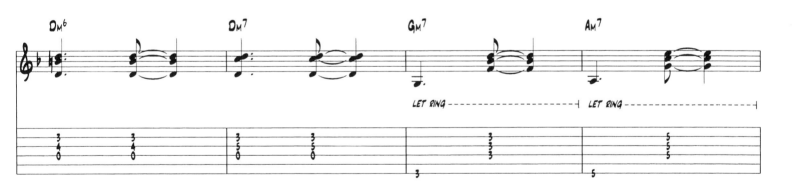

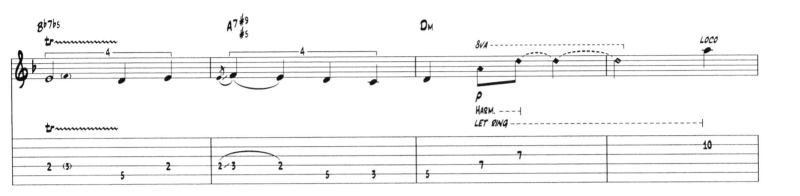

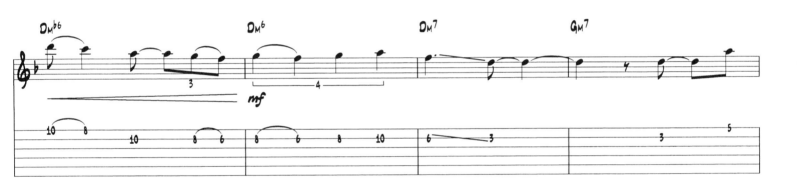

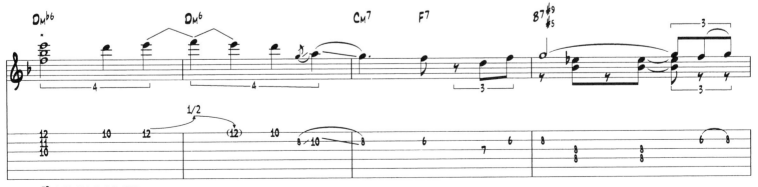

*Played behind the beat.

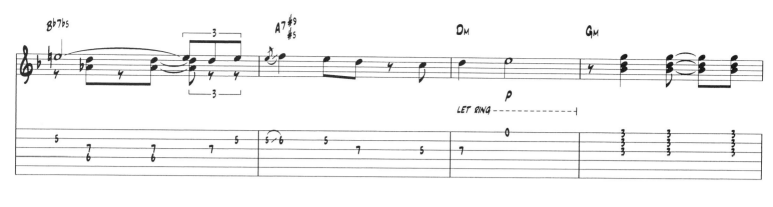

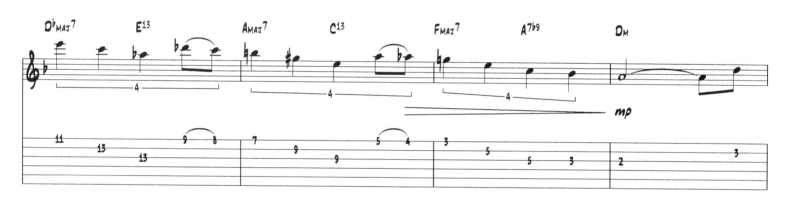

*Played behind the beat.

Pitch: E

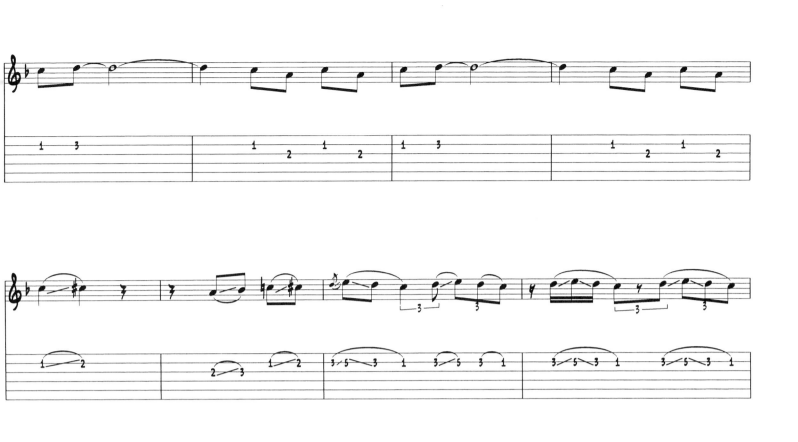

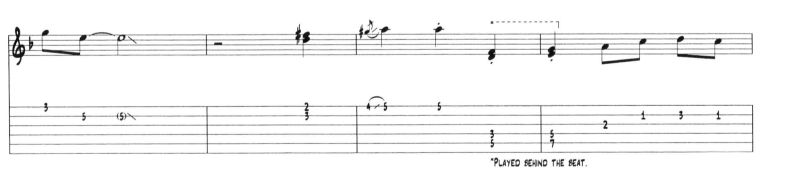

*PLAYED BEHIND THE BEAT.

*Music sounds in normal octave.

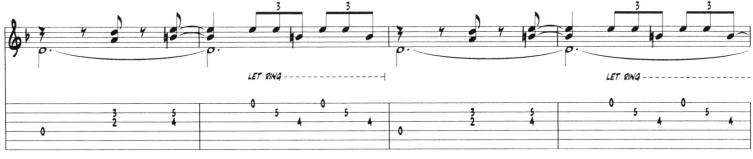

**One octave higher.

***Normal octave

*ONE OCTAVE HIGHER.

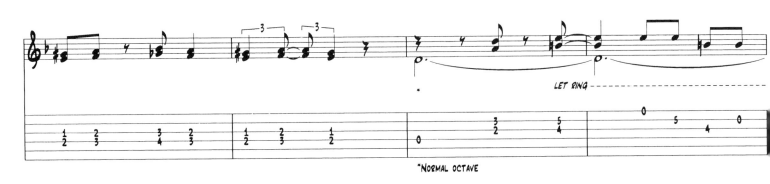

*Normal octave

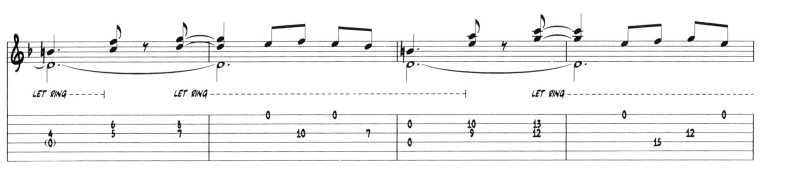

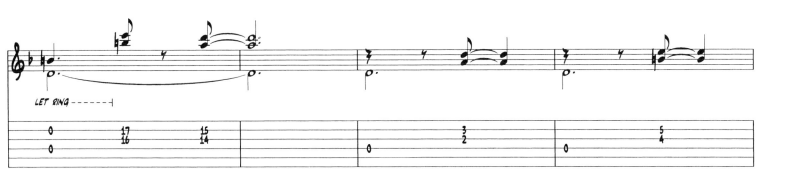

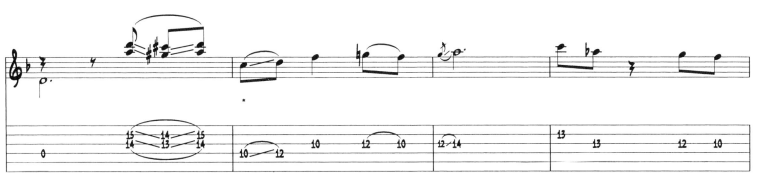

*One octave higher.

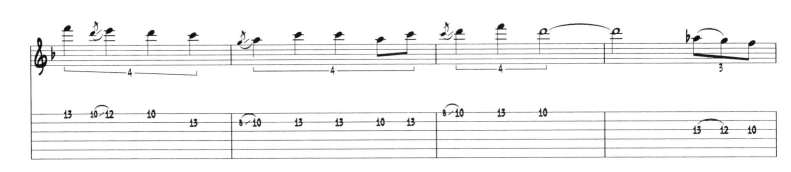

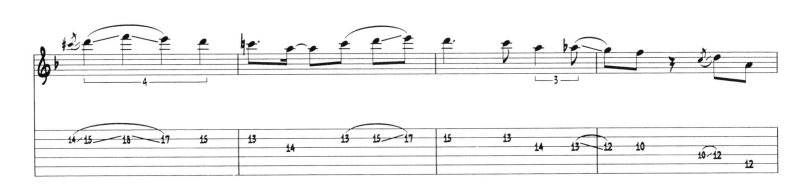

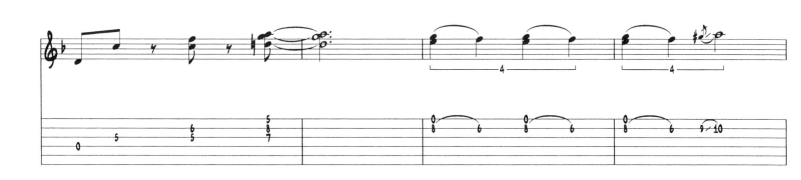

LET RING -

43

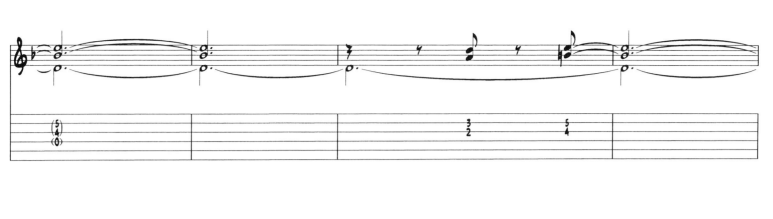

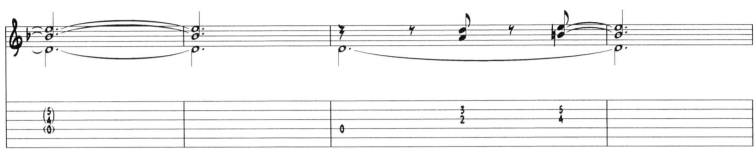

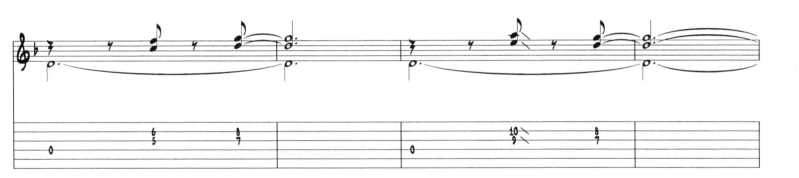

*Synth. gtr. frenzy. next 18 meas. Rhythm and Pitches are approximate.

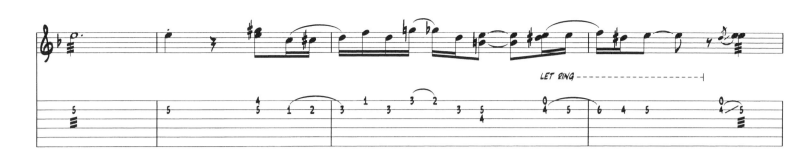

LET RING -

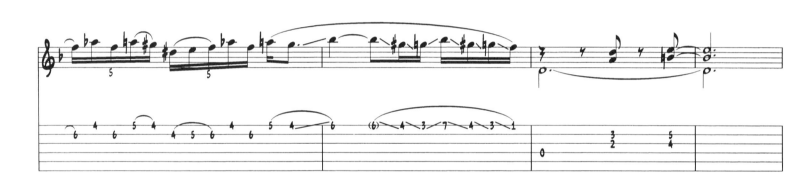

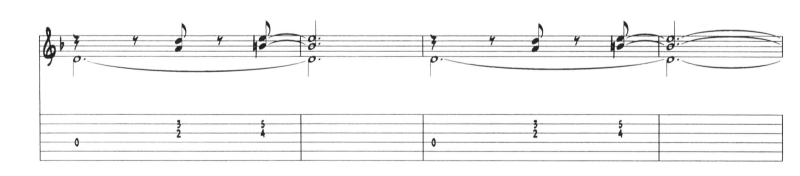

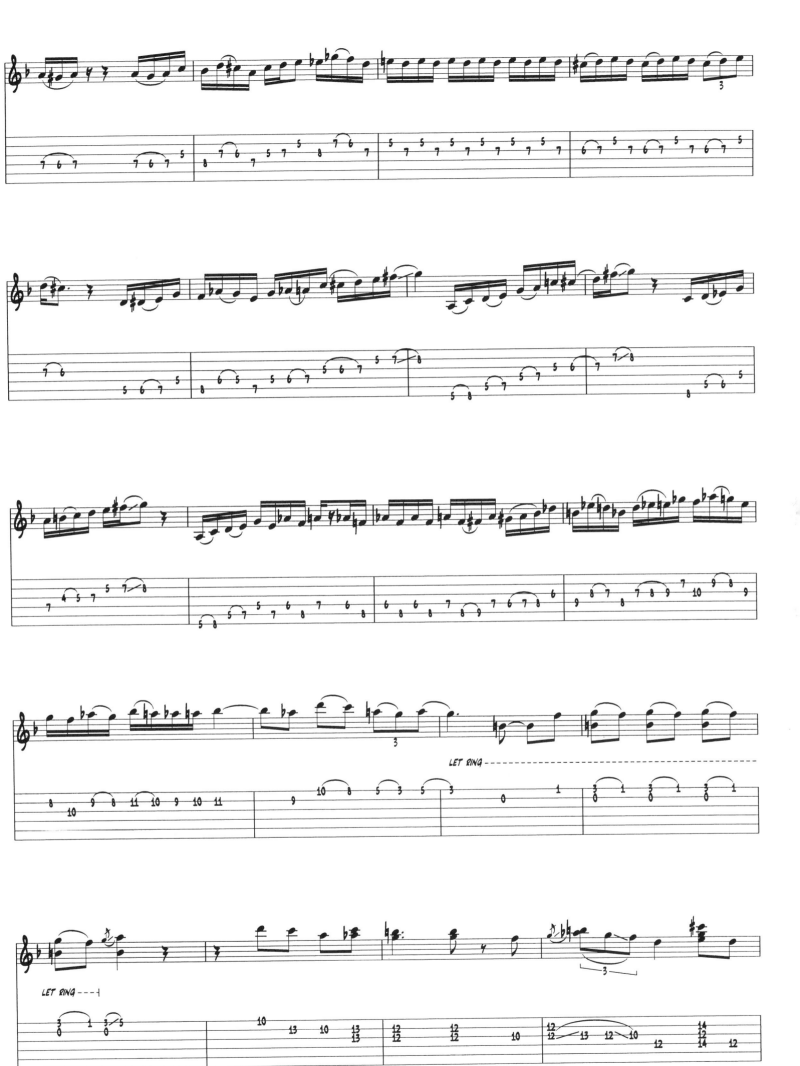

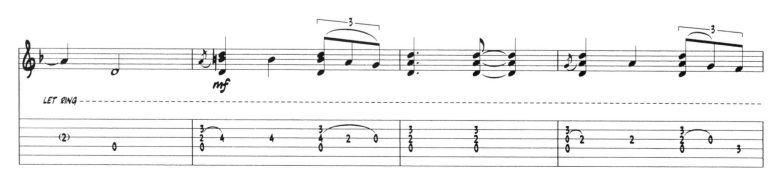

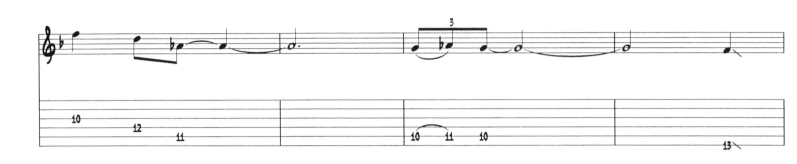

*SYNTH. GTR. FRENZY AS BEFORE. NEXT 22 MEAS.

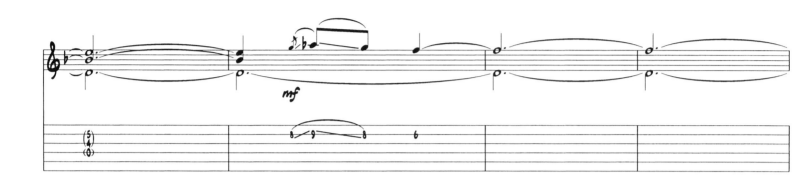

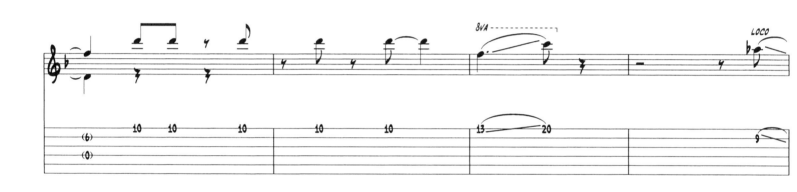

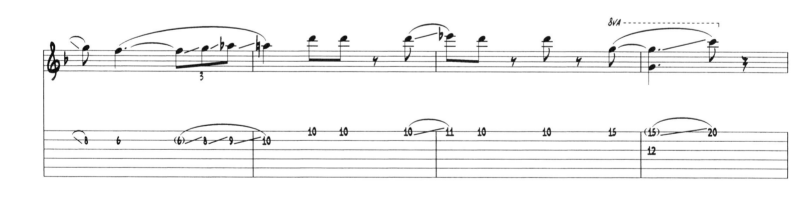

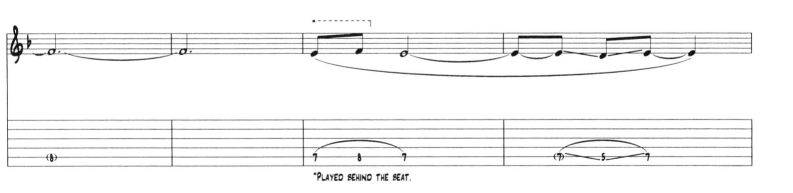

*Played behind the beat.

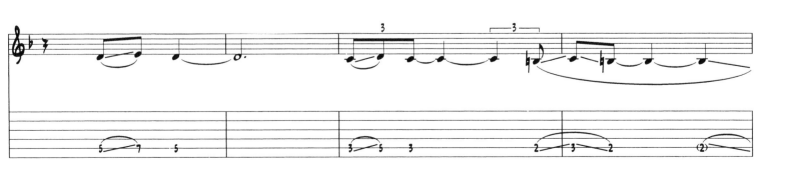

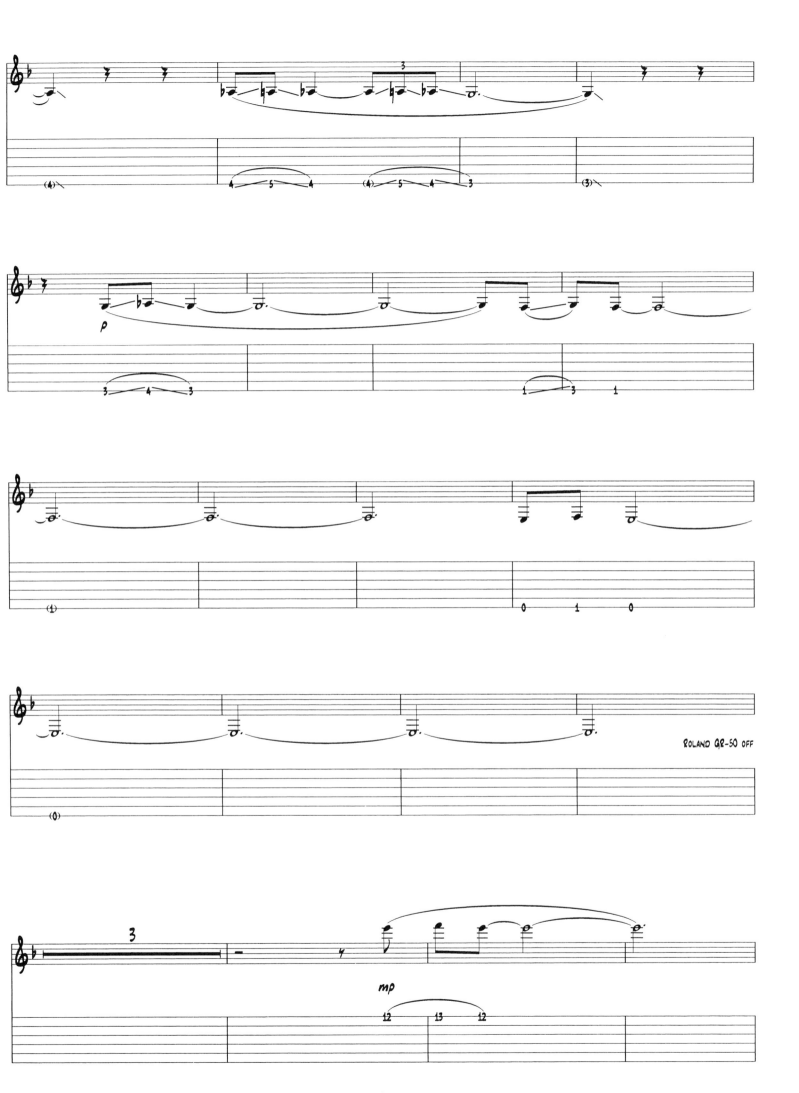

ROLAND GR-50 OFF

55

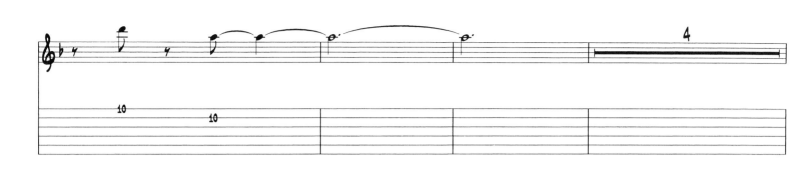
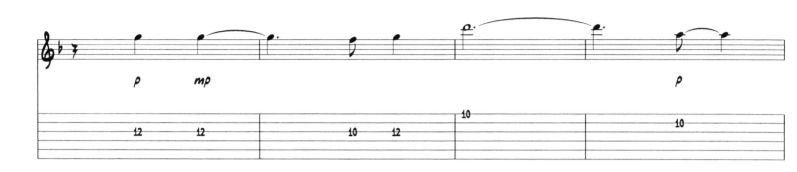
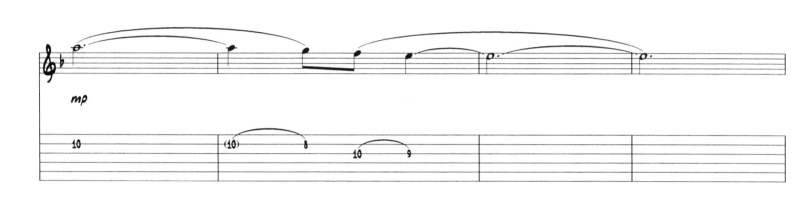

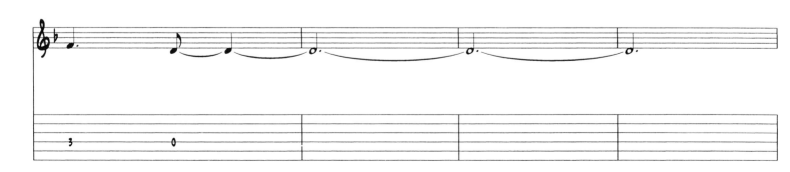

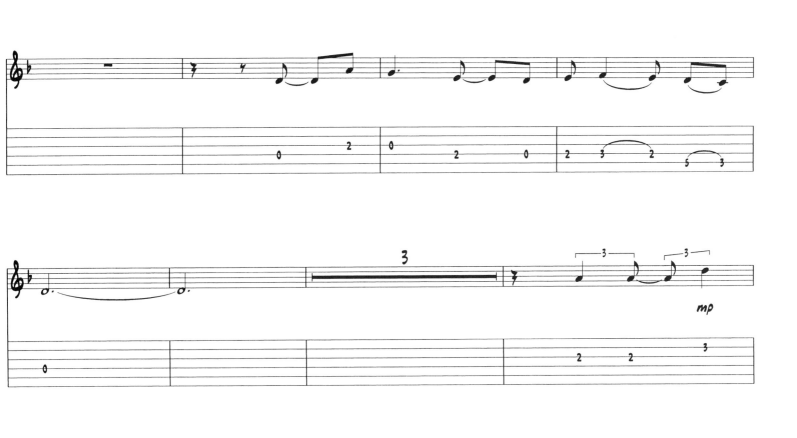

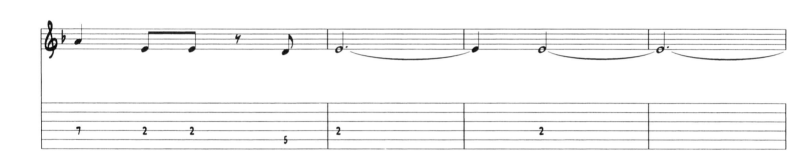

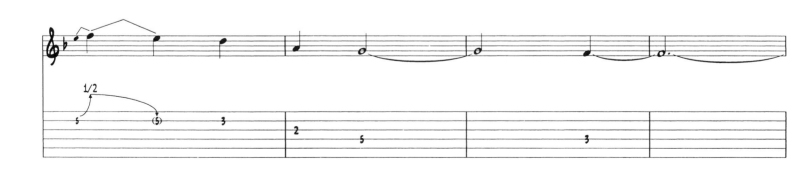

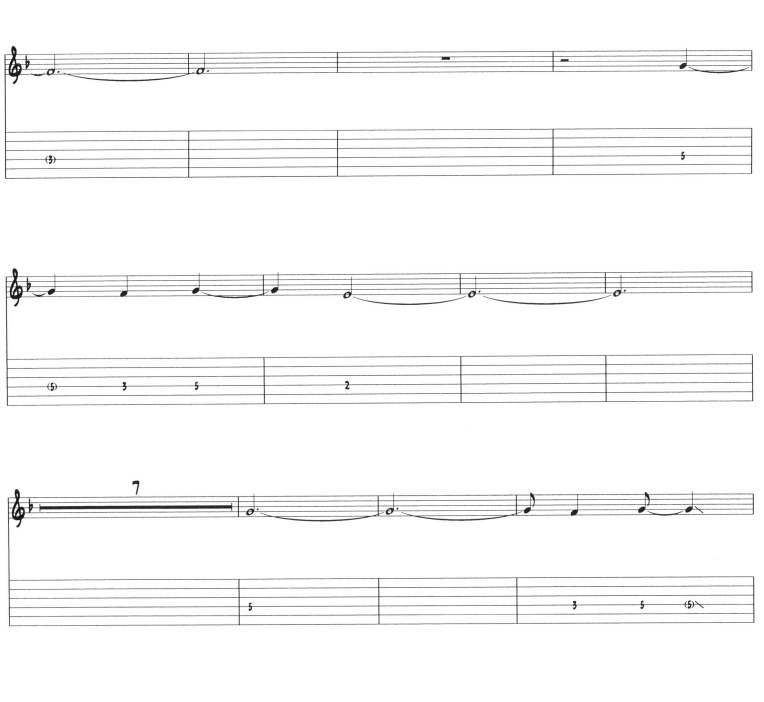

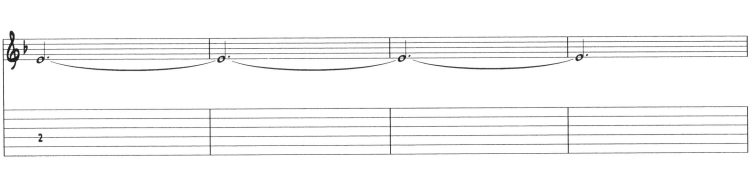

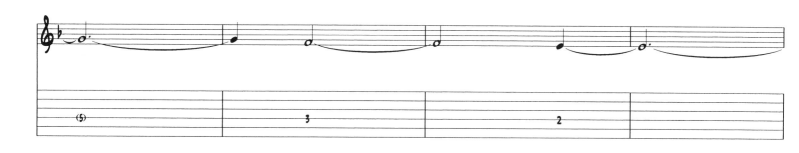

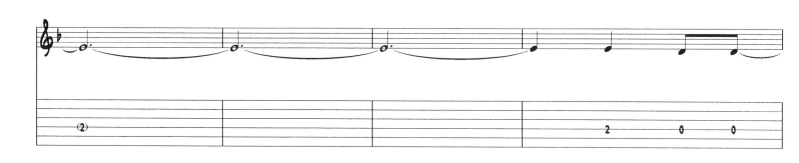

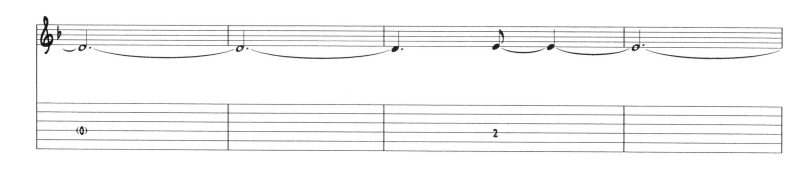

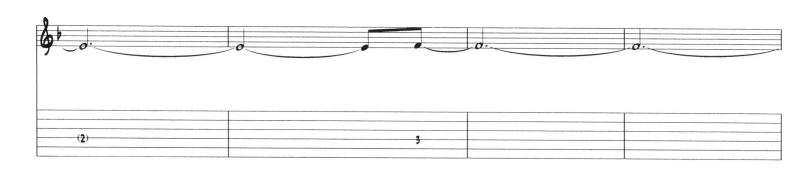

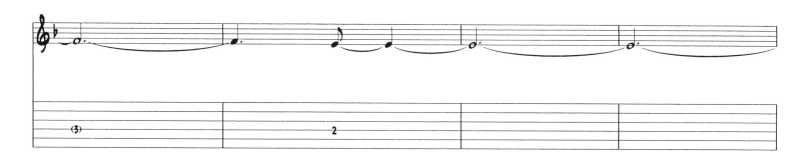

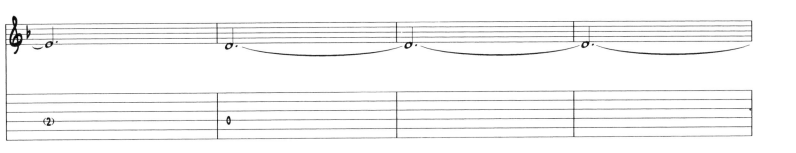

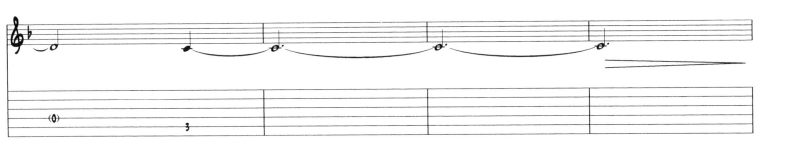

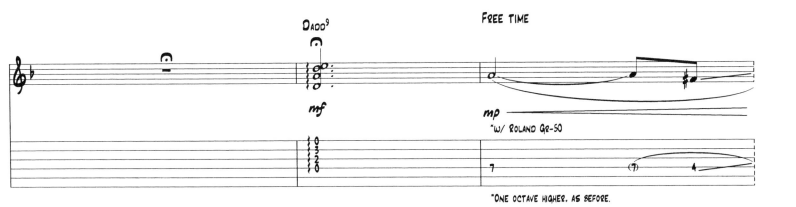

*One octave higher, as before.

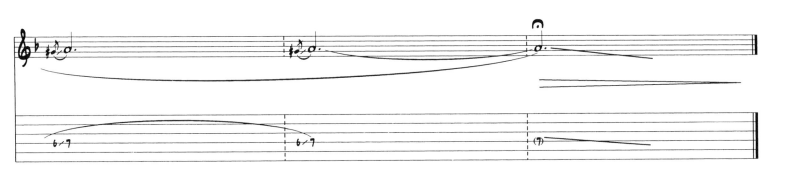

Giant Steps

By John Coltrane

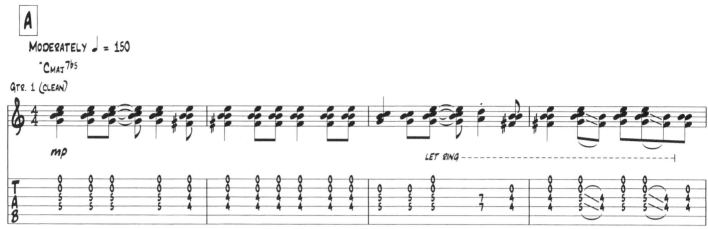

*Chord symbols reflect basic harmony.

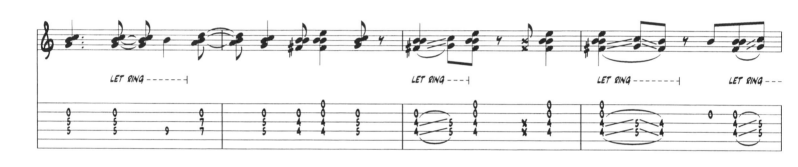

*Played behind the beat.

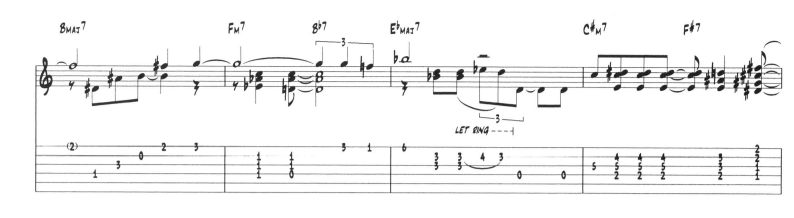

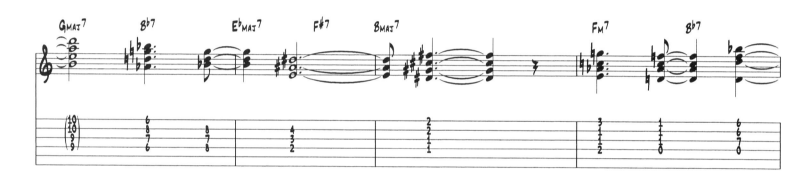

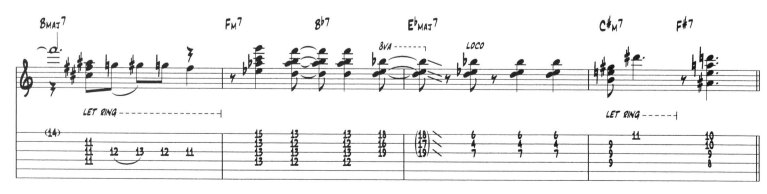

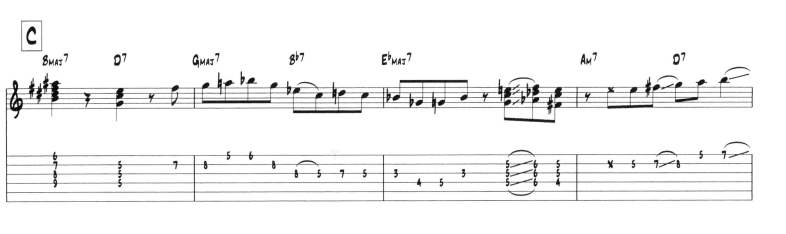

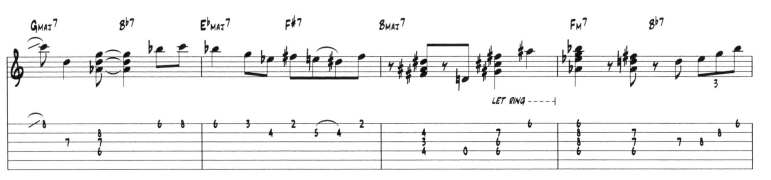

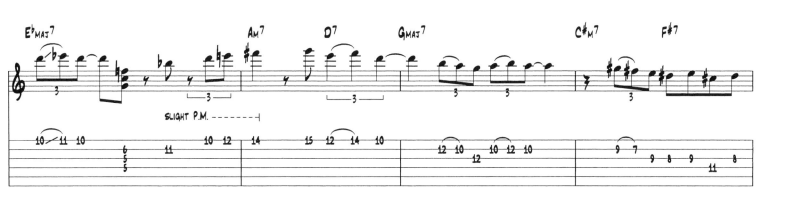

*Played behind the beat. Next 3 meas.

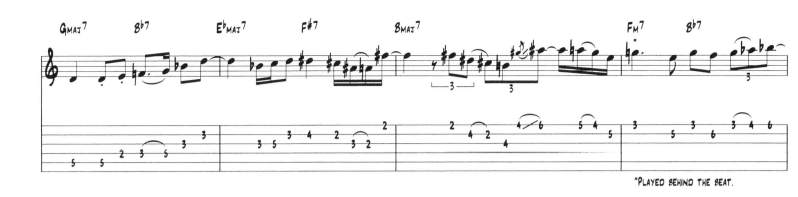

*Played behind the beat.

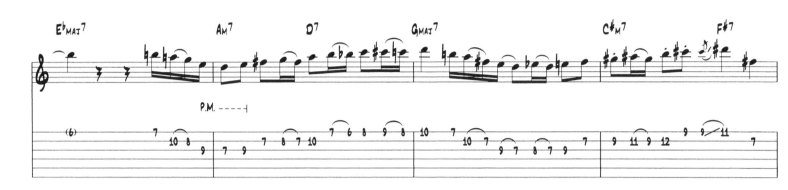

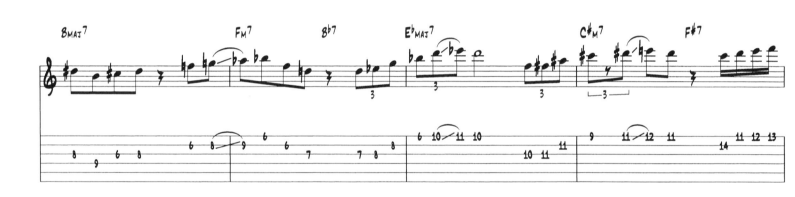

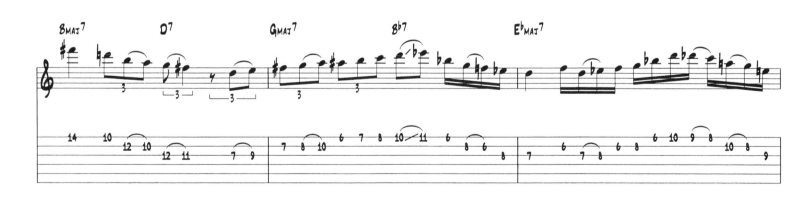

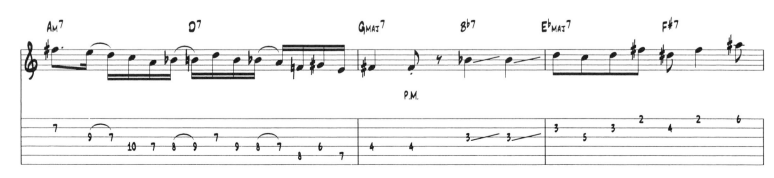

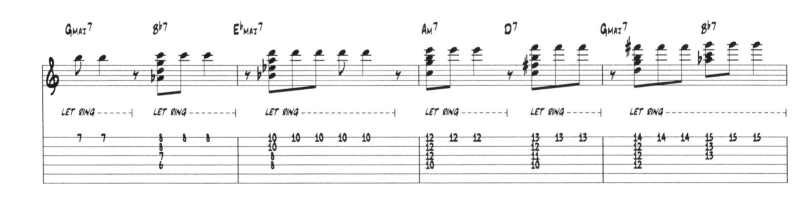

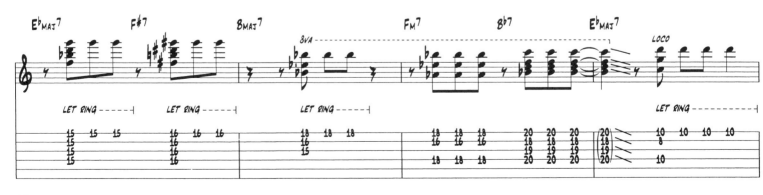

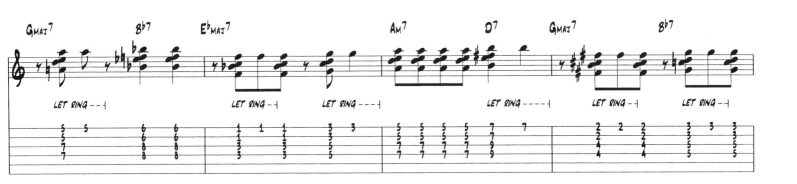

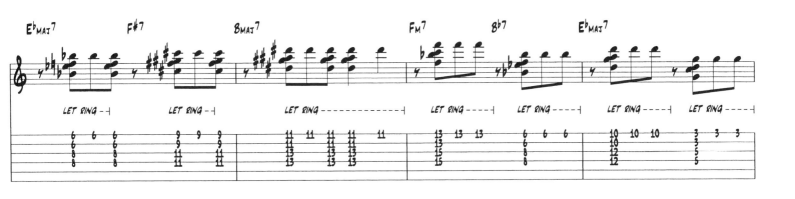

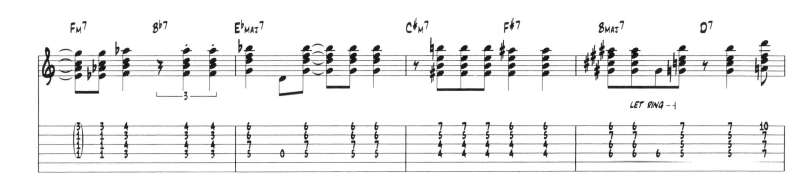

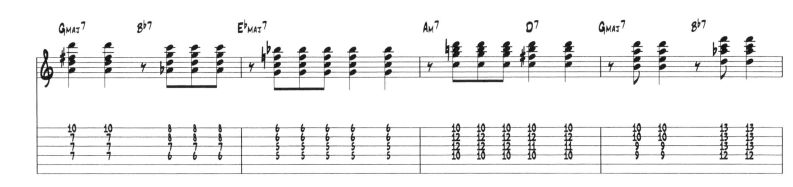

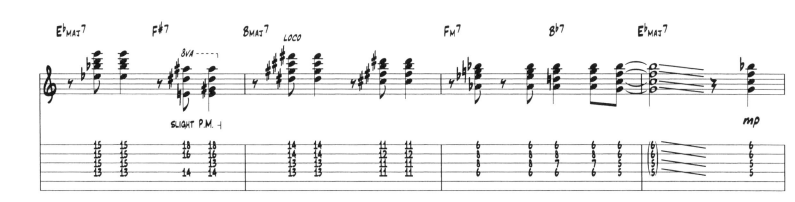

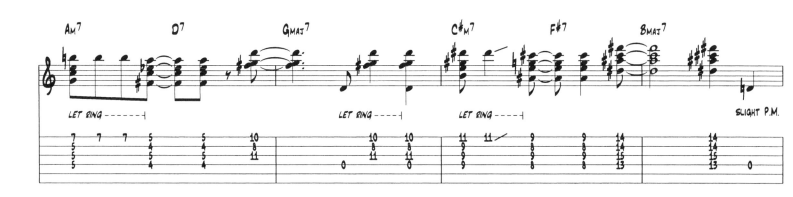

*Played behind the beat.

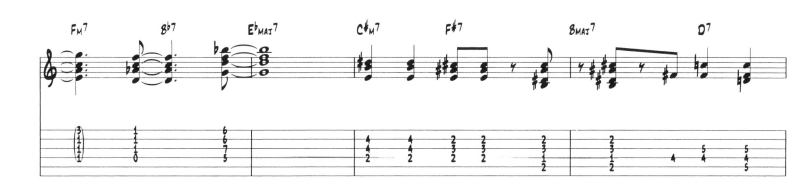

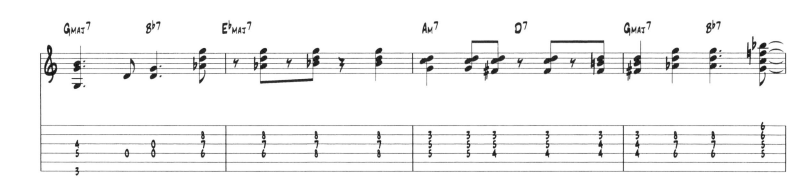

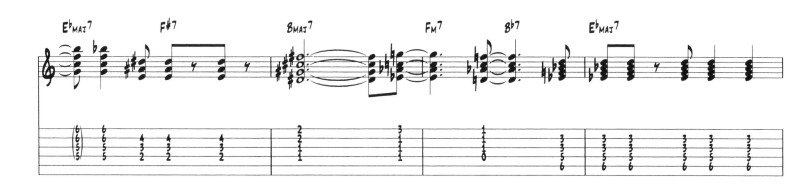

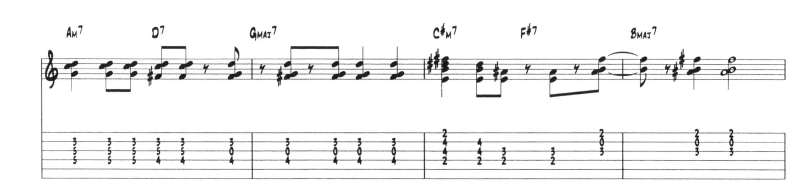

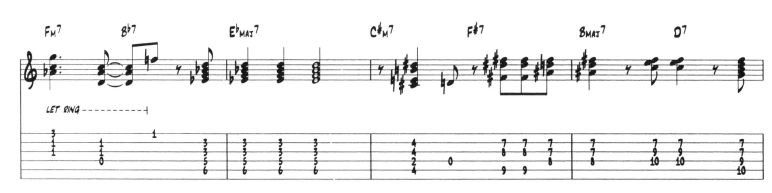

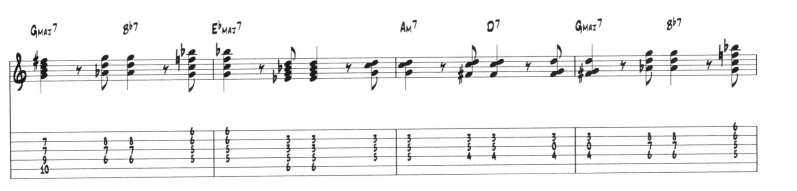

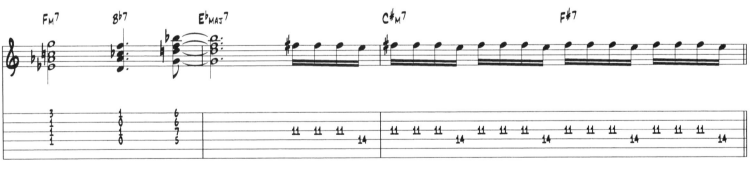

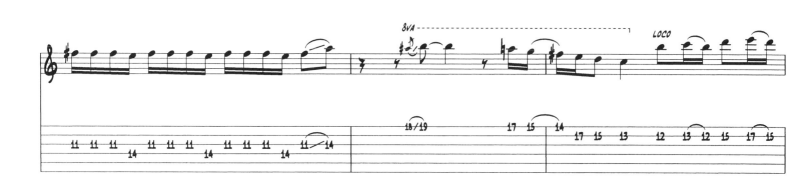
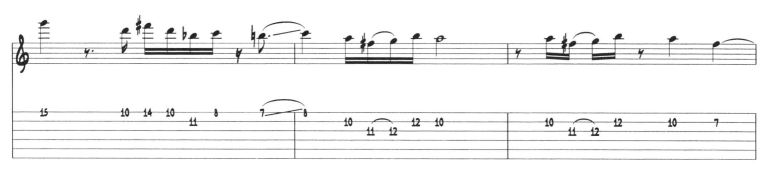

*Played behind the beat.

80

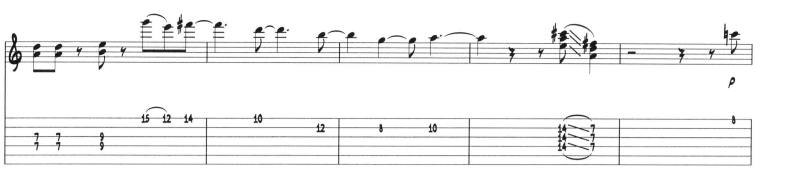

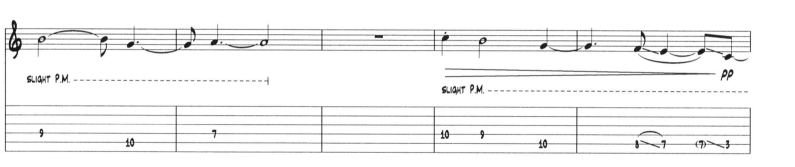
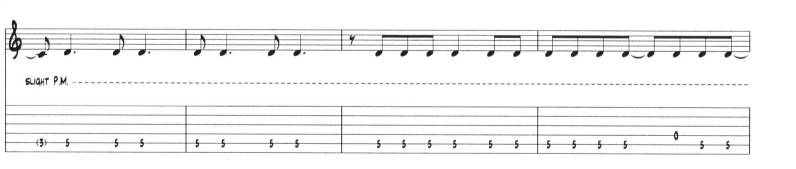

Into the Dream

By Pat Metheny

*42-str. Pikaso gtr. arr. for acous. gtrs.
**Chord symbols reflect implied harmony.

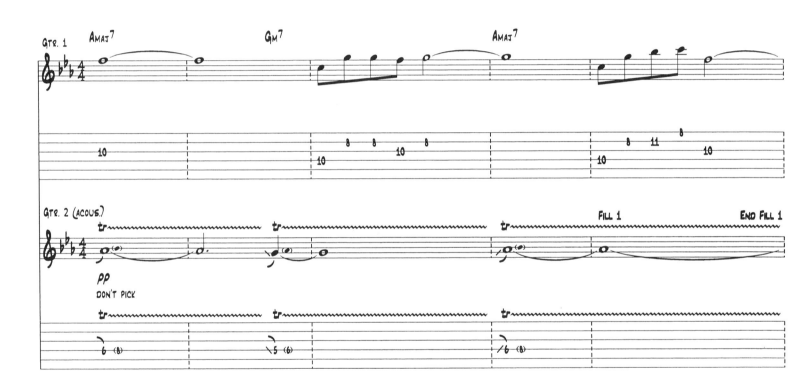

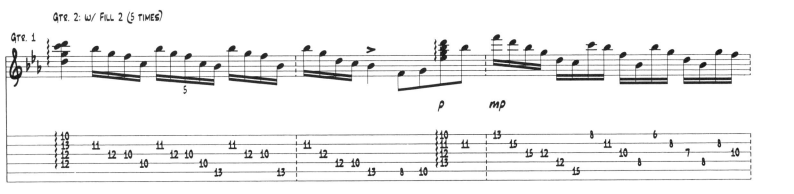

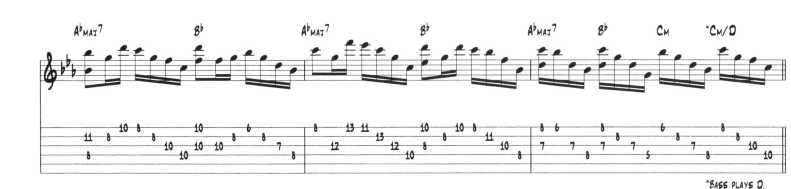

*Bass plays D.

B

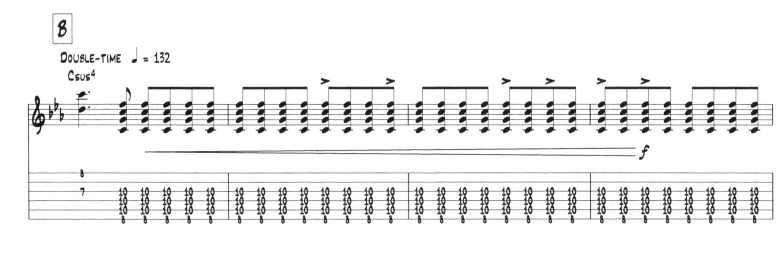

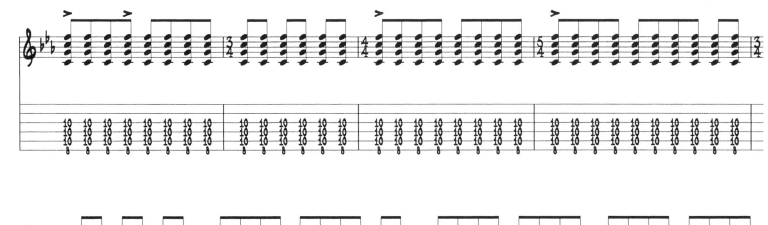

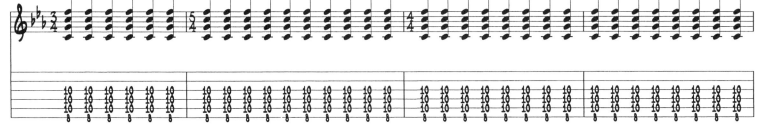

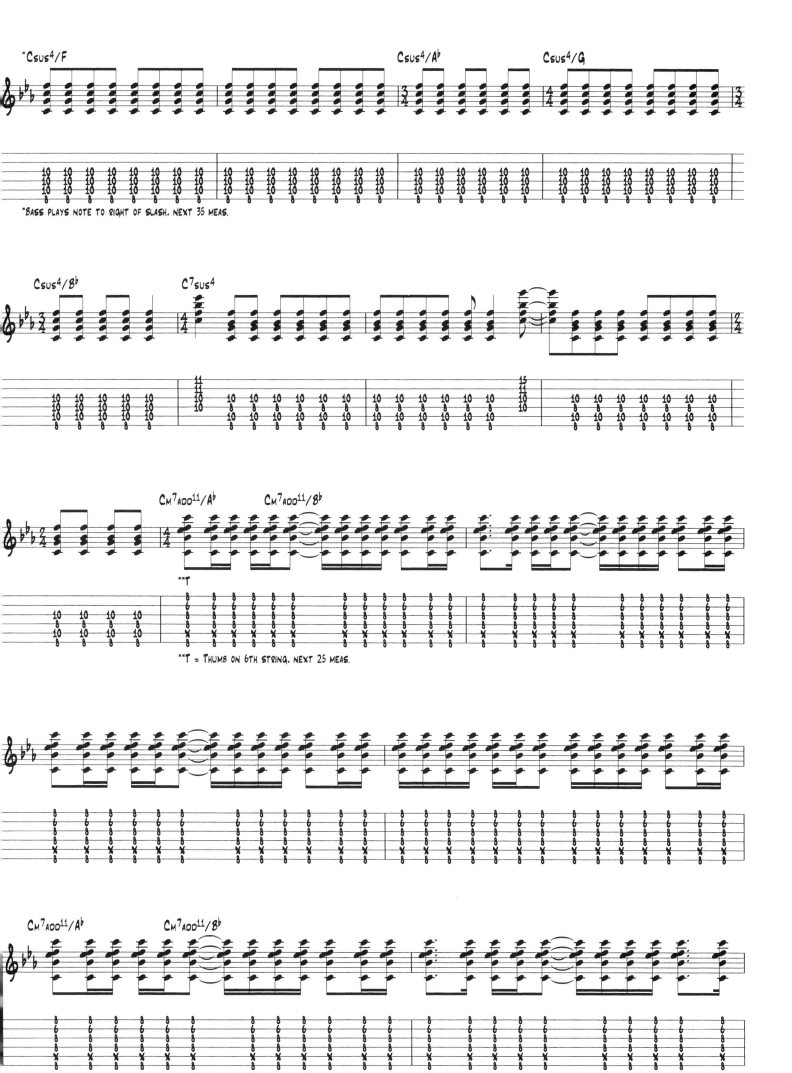

*BASS PLAYS NOTE TO RIGHT OF SLASH. NEXT 35 MEAS.

**T = THUMB ON 6TH STRING. NEXT 25 MEAS.

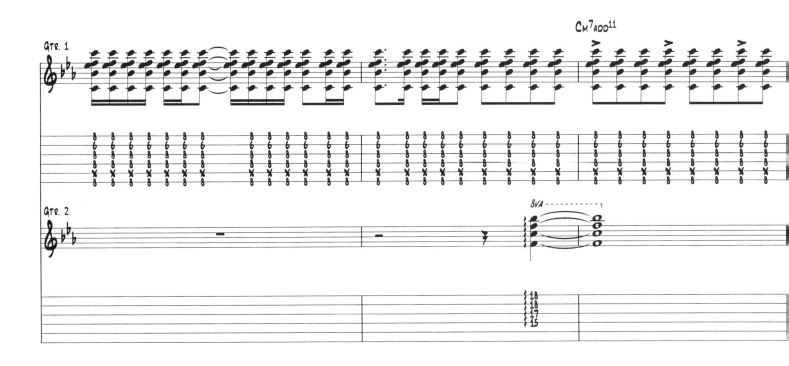

Gtr. 2 tacet

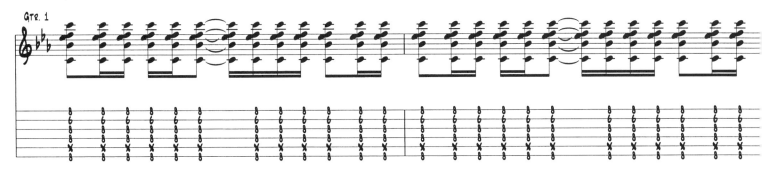

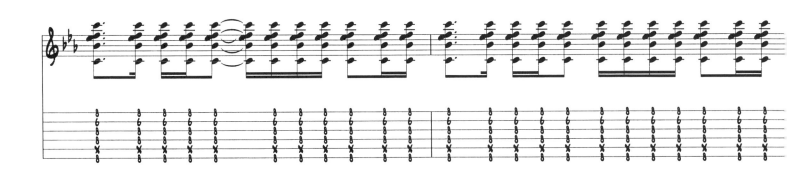

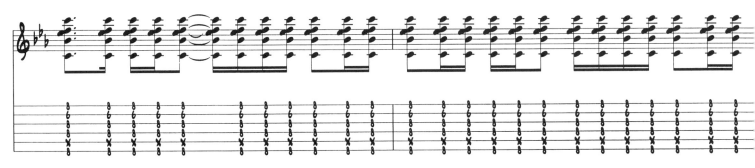

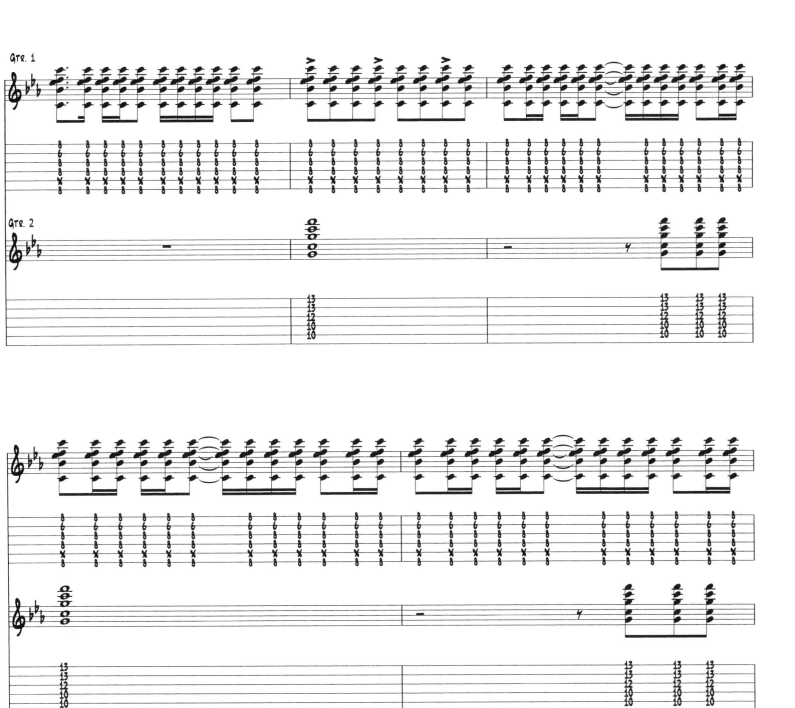
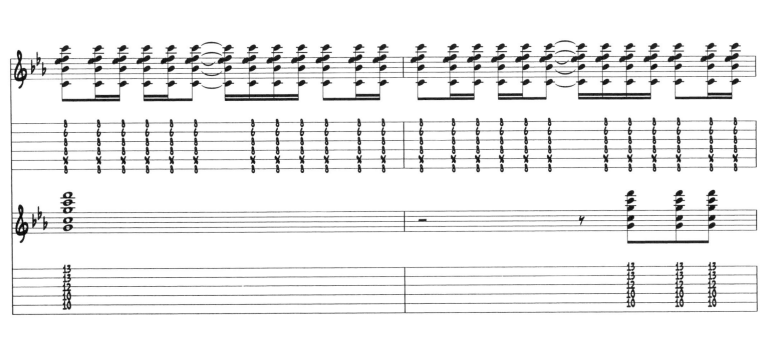

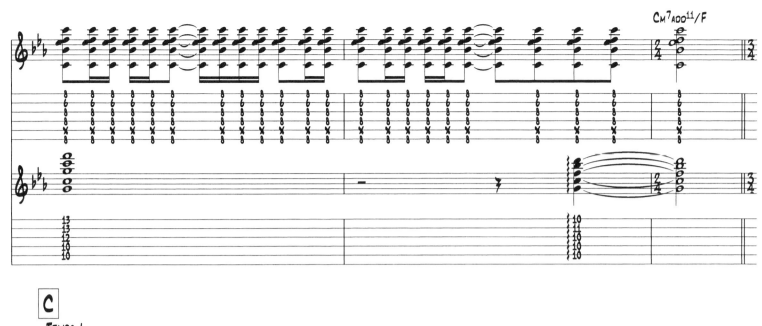

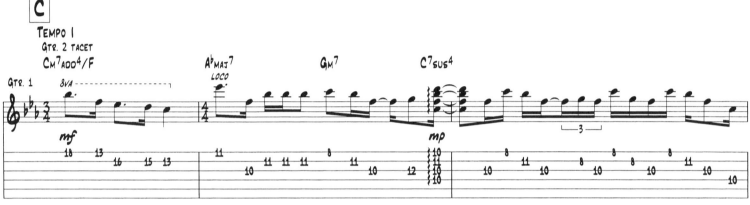

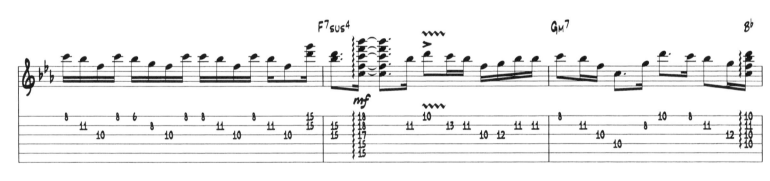

Segue to "So May It Secretly Begin"

So May It Secretly Begin

By Pat Metheny

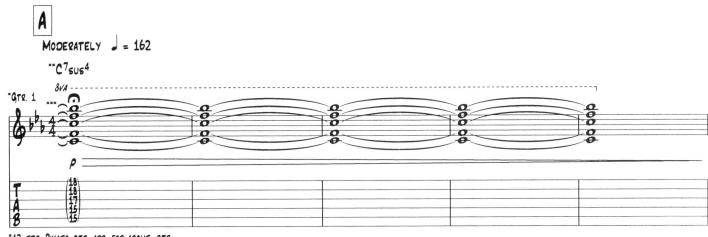

*42-str. Pikaso gtr. arr. for acous. gtr.
**Chord symbols reflect overall harmony.
***Tied from "Into the Dream."

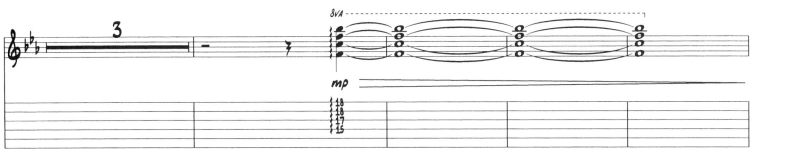

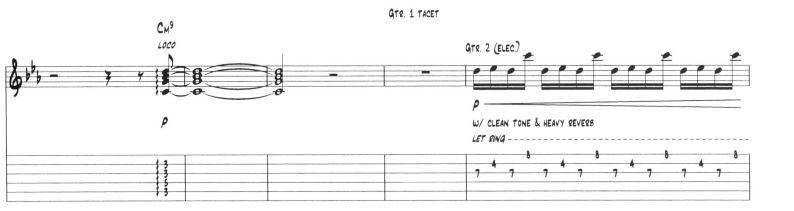

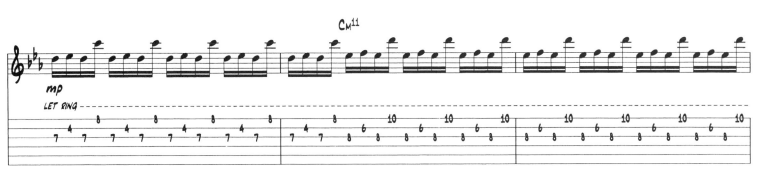

*CHORD SYMBOLS REFLECT BASIC HARMONY.

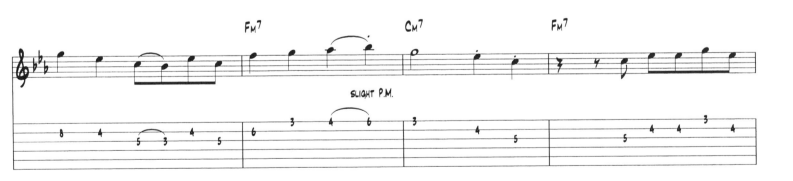

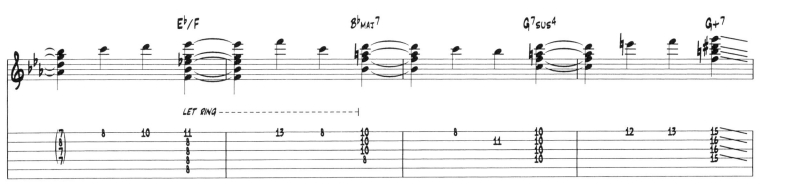

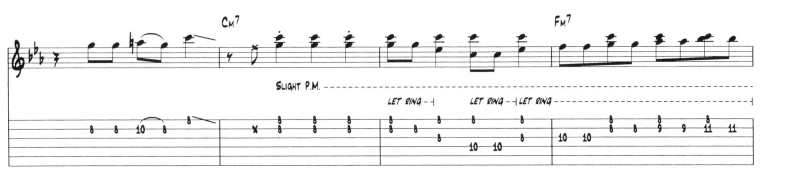

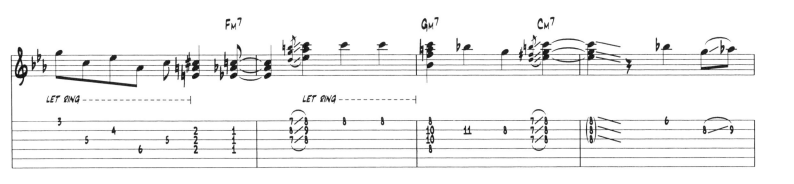

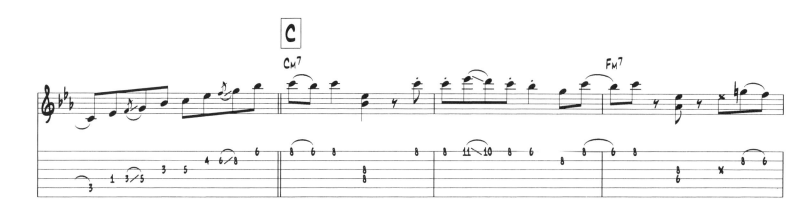

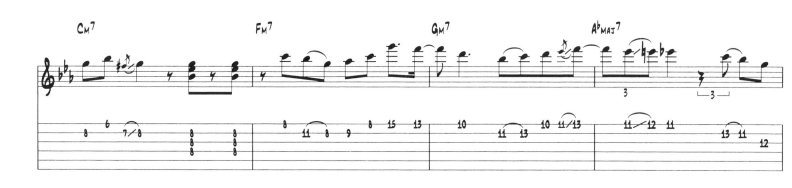

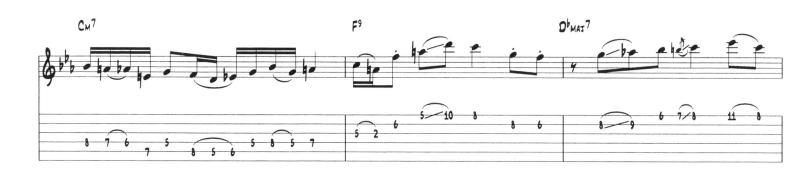

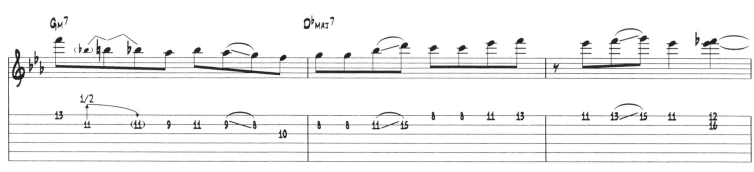

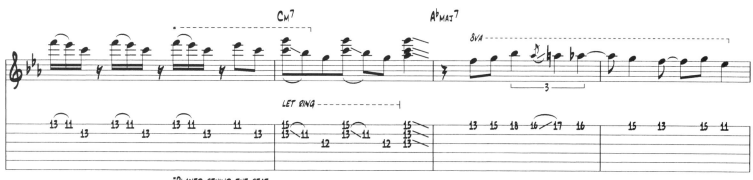

*Played behind the beat.

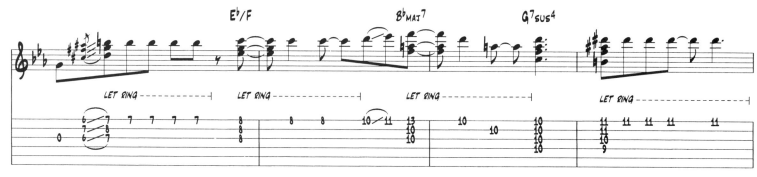

*Played behind the beat.

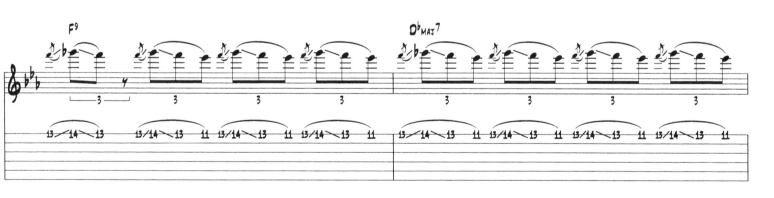

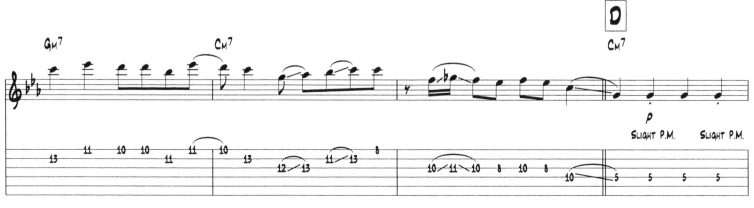

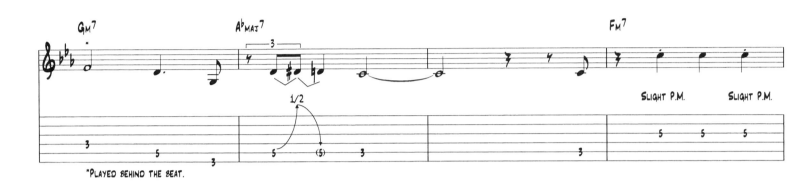

*Played behind the beat.

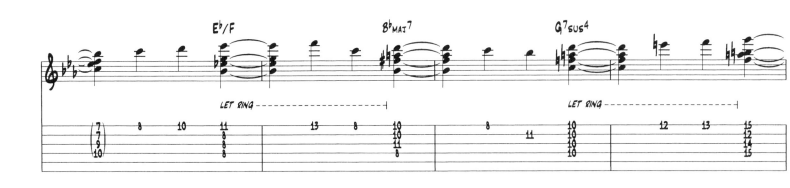

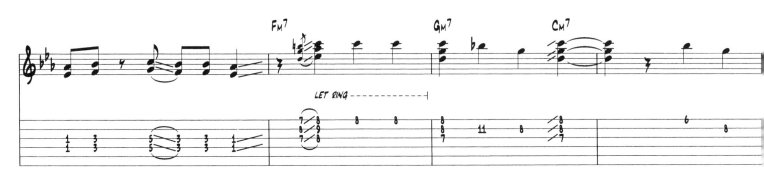

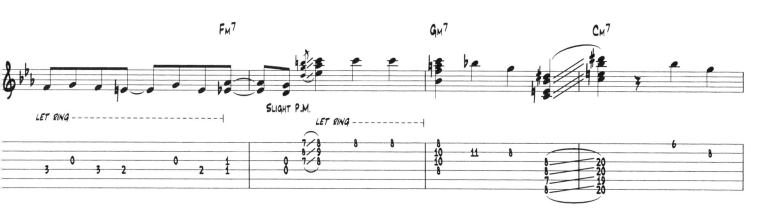
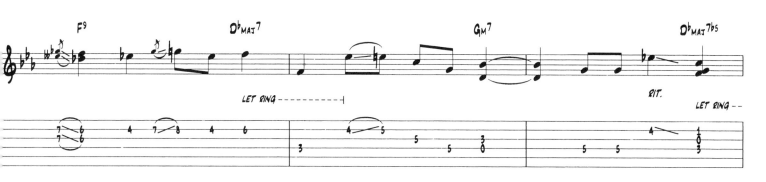

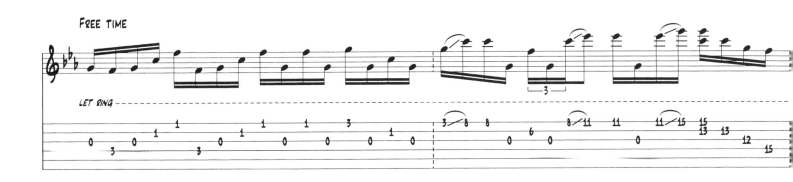

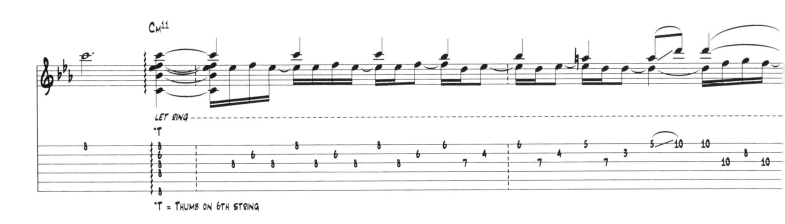

"T = Thumb on 6th string

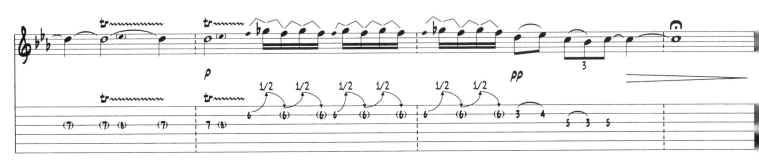

The Bat

By Pat Metheny

*Chord symbols reflect overall harmony.

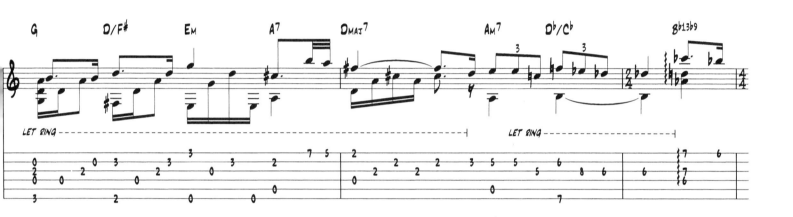

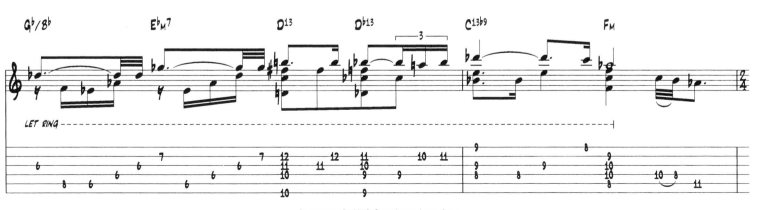

103

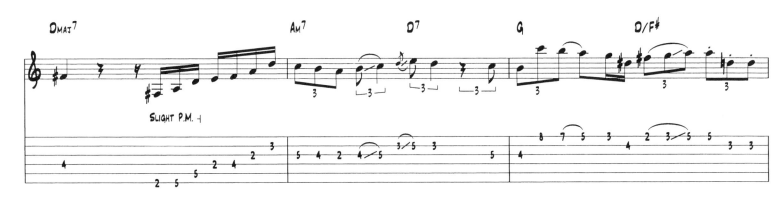

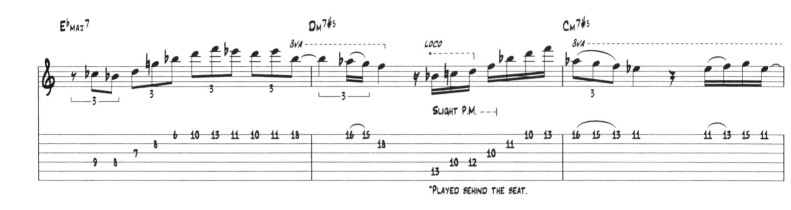

*Played behind the beat.

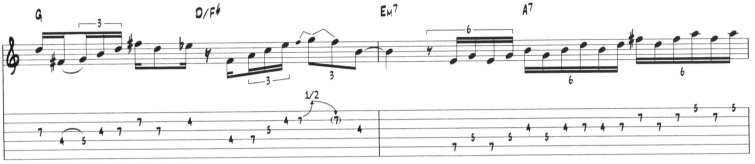

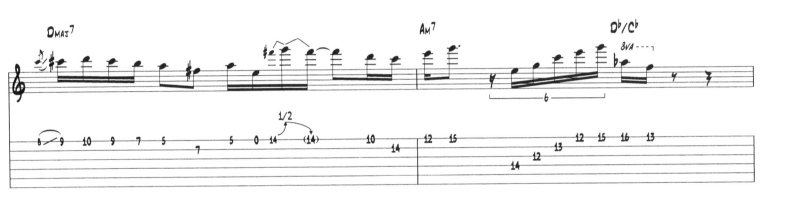

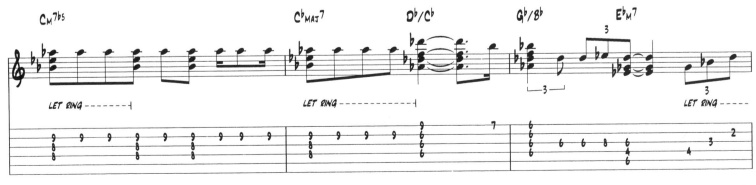

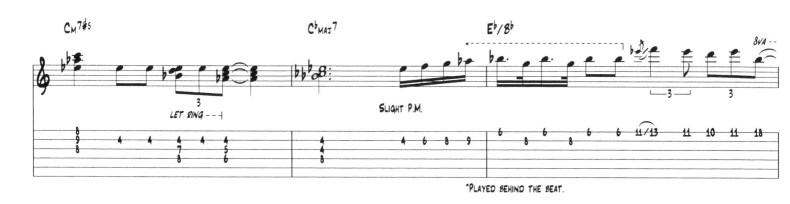

*Played behind the beat.

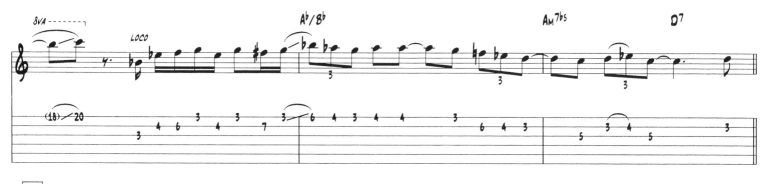

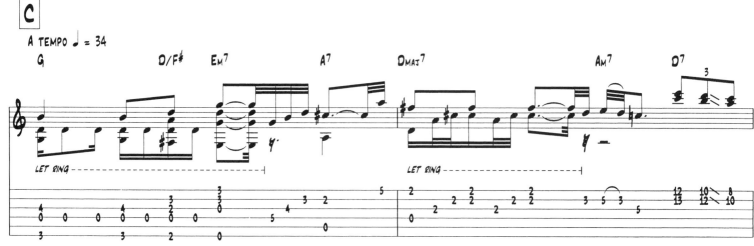

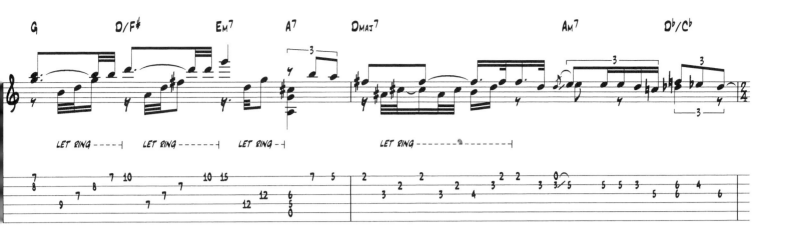

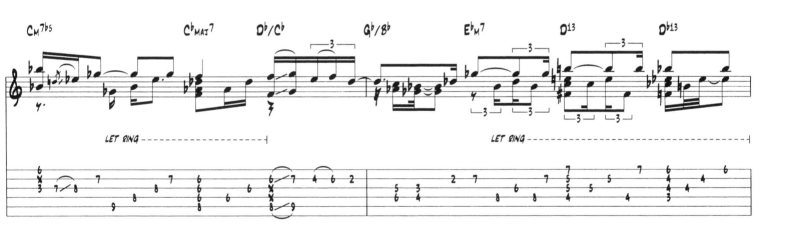

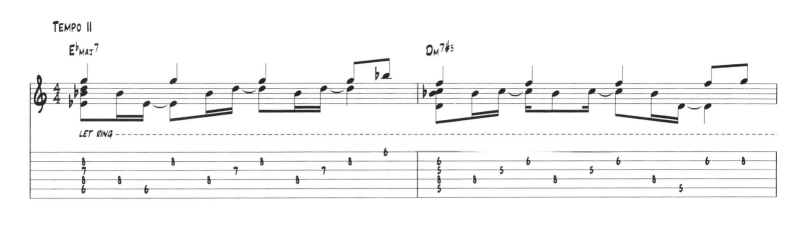

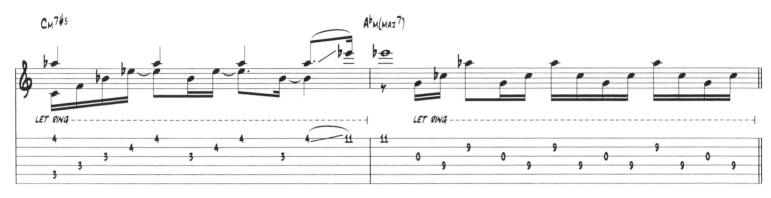

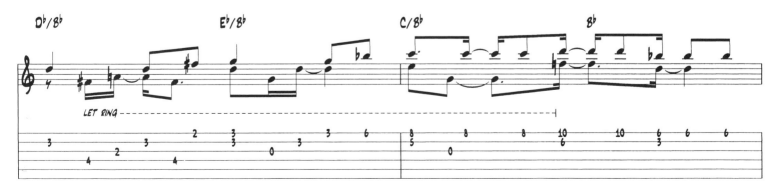

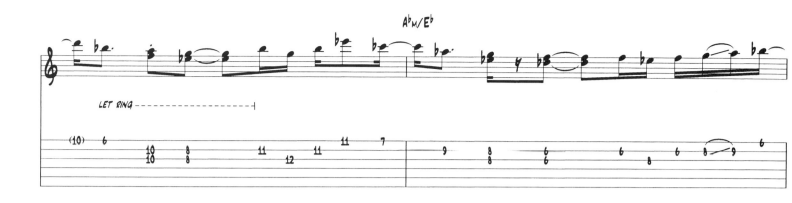

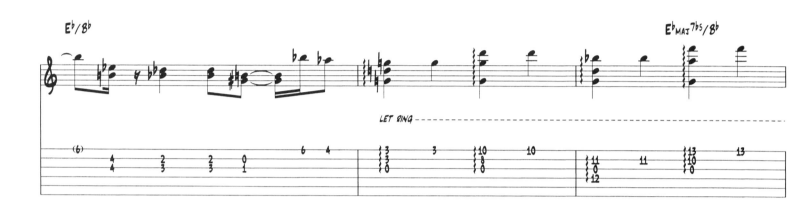

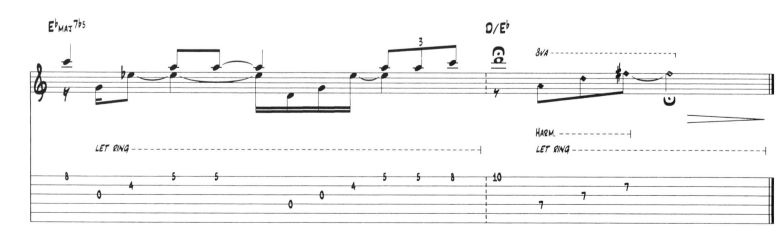

All the Things You Are

Lyrics by Oscar Hammerstein II
Music by Jerome Kern

*Chord symbols reflect implied harmony.

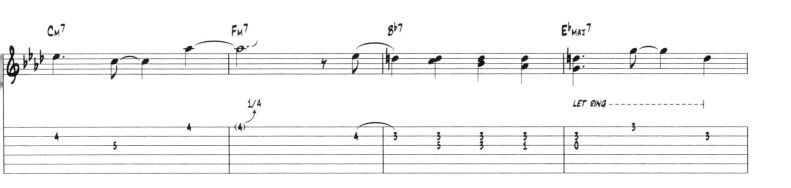

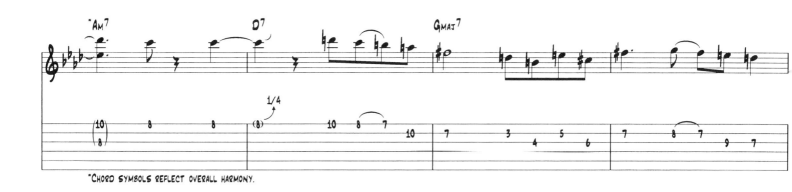

*Chord symbols reflect overall harmony.

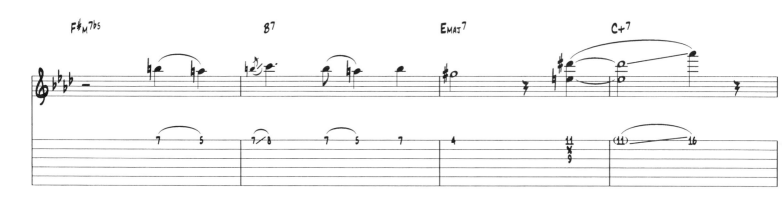

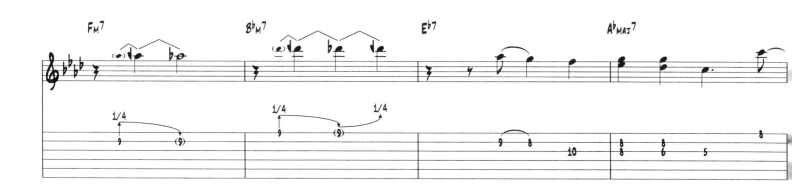

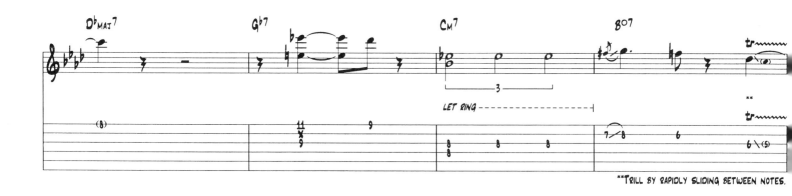

**Trill by rapidly sliding between notes.

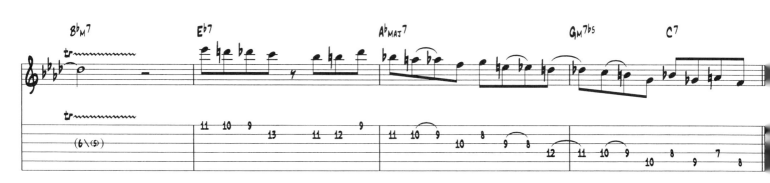

116

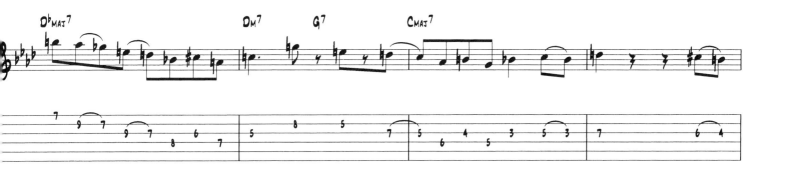

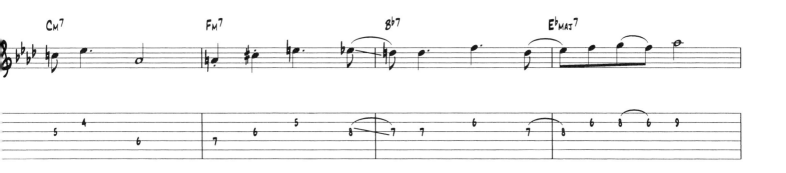

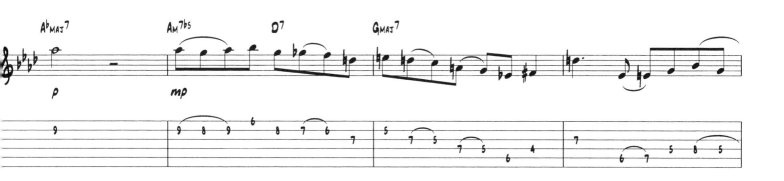

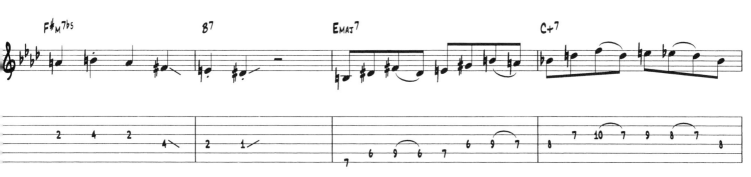

117

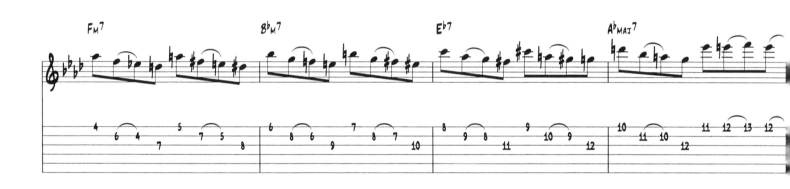

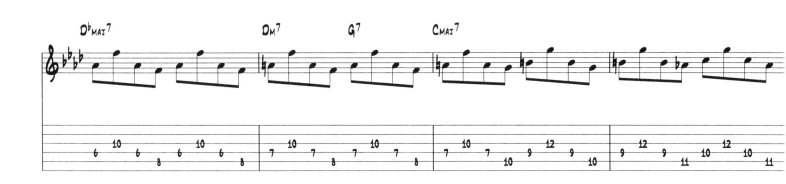

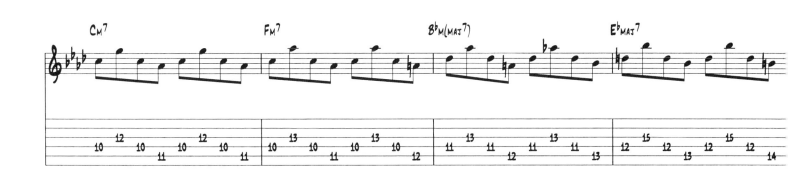

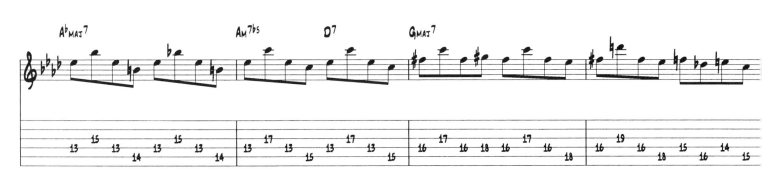

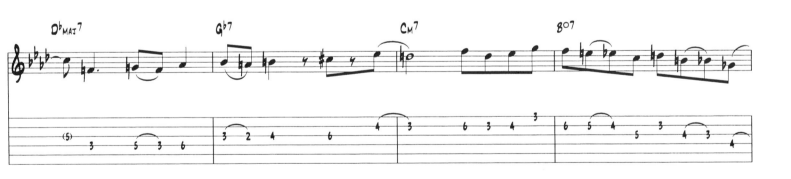

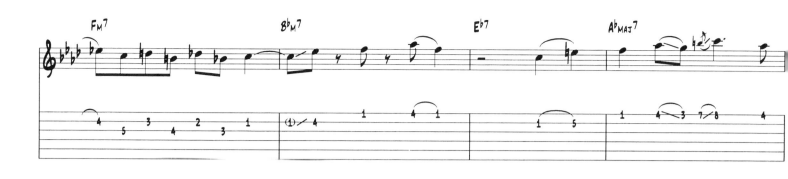

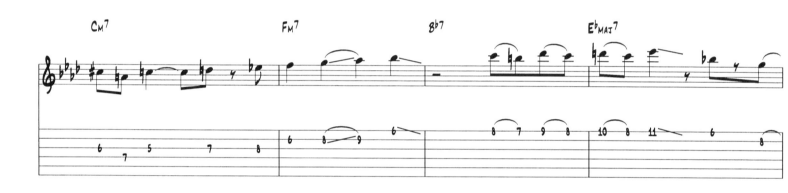

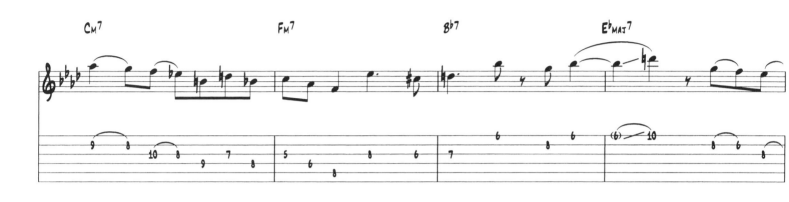

126

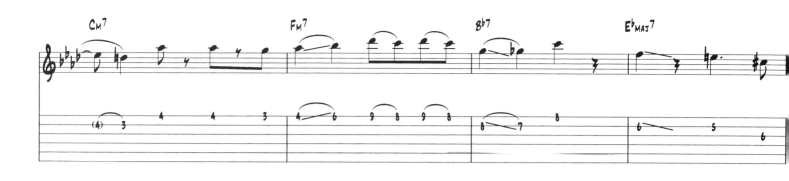

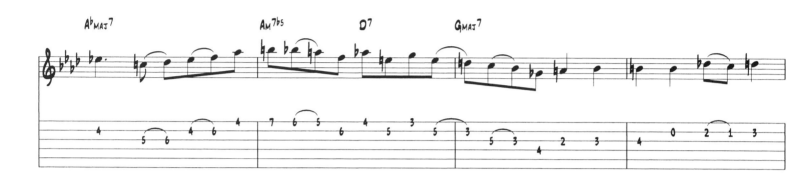

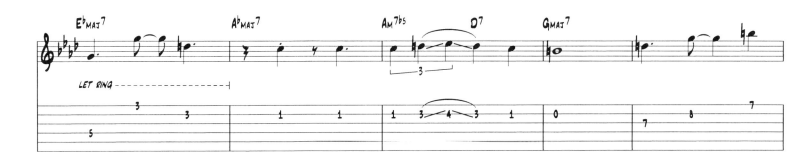

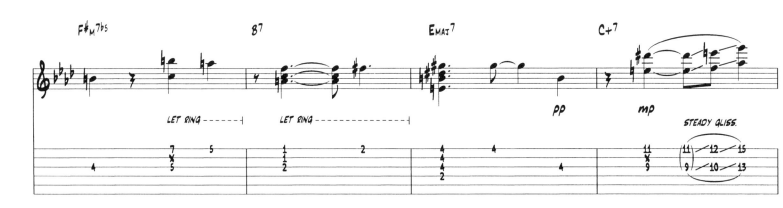

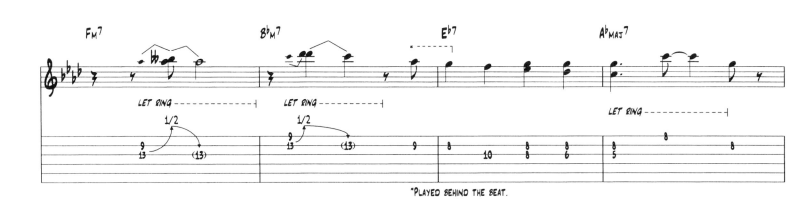

*Played behind the beat.

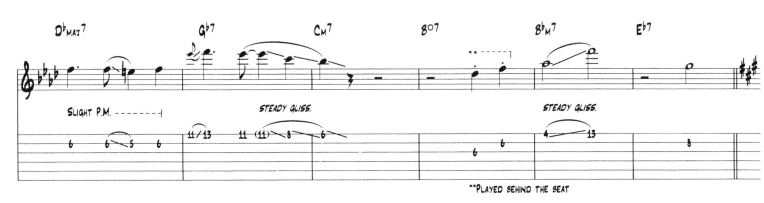

**Played behind the beat

*Played behind the beat.

SLIGHT P.M. --

SLIGHT P.M. --

SLIGHT P.M. ------------------------------

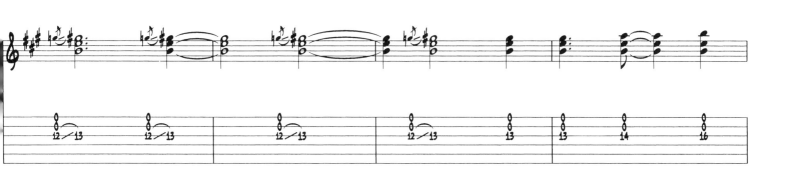

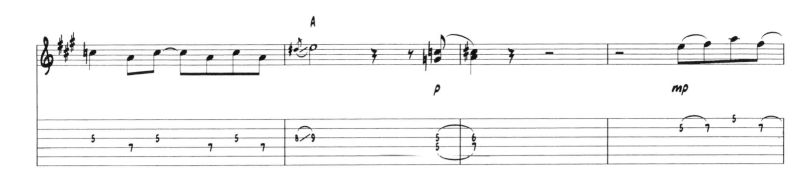

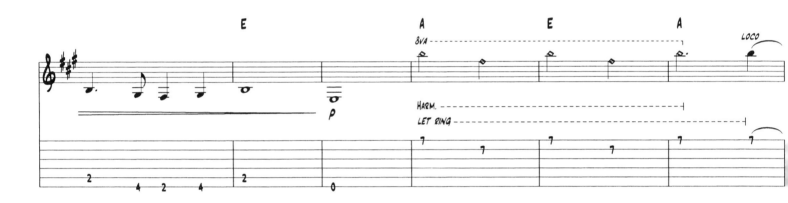

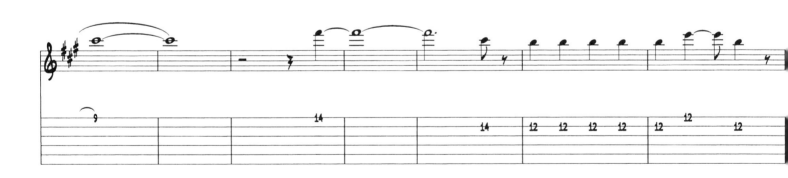

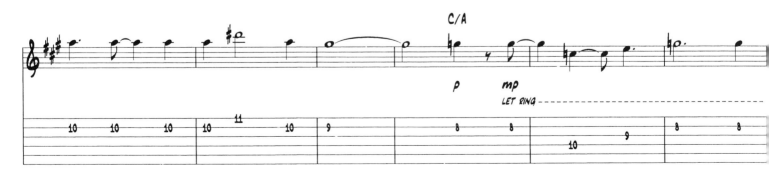

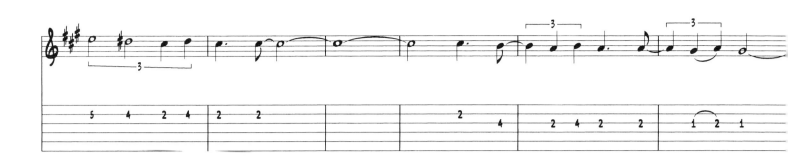

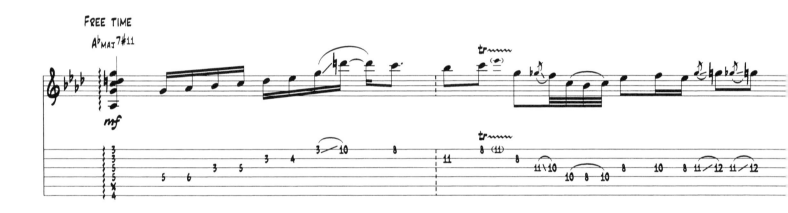
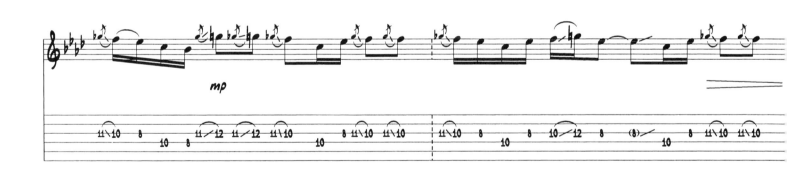

138

James

By Pat Metheny and Lyle Mays

Drop D tuning:
(low to high) D-A-D-G-B-E

*Chord symbols reflect basic harmony.

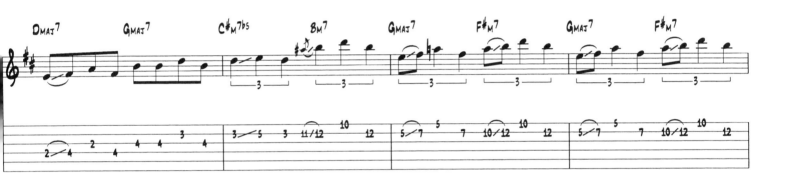

**Played behind the beat.

*Played behind the beat

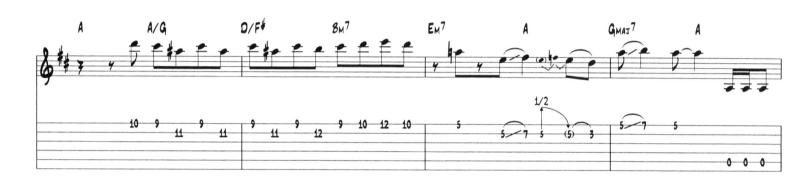

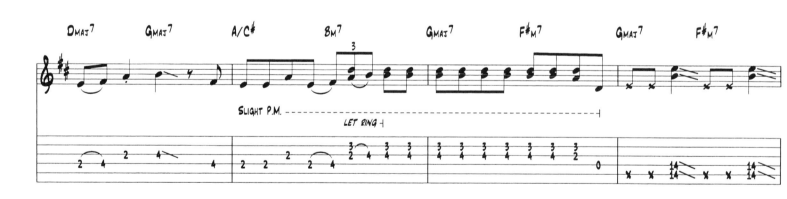

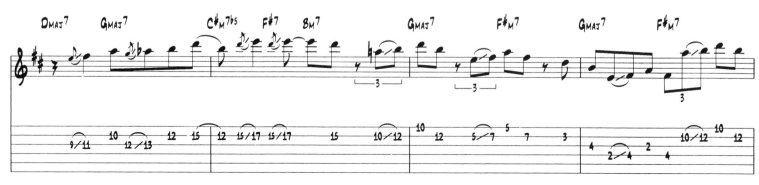

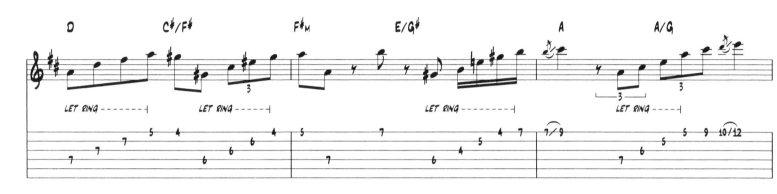

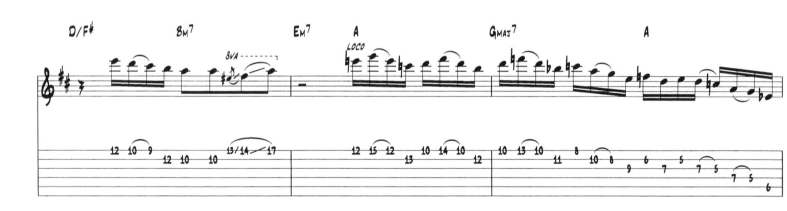

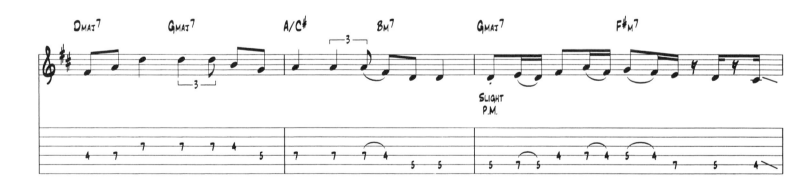

142

143

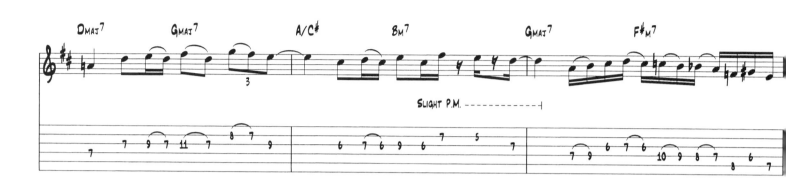

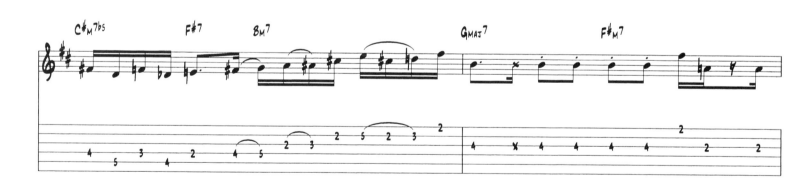

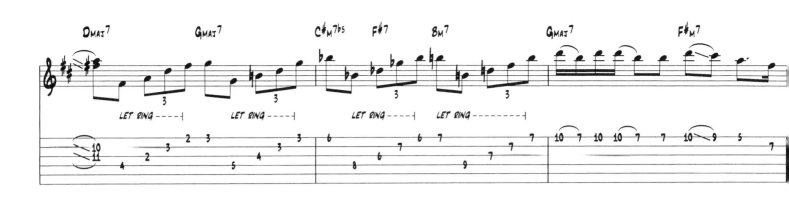
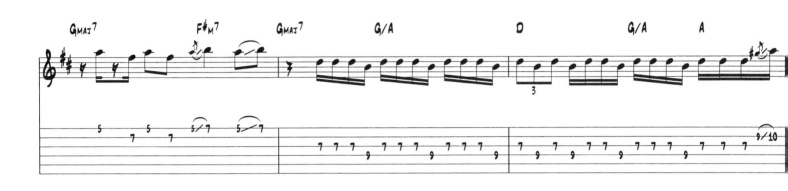
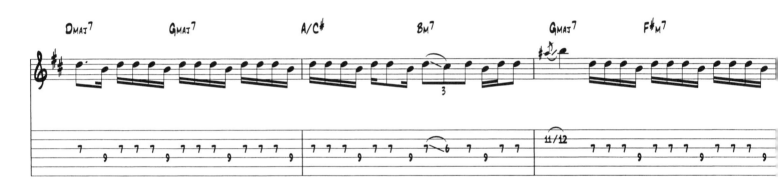
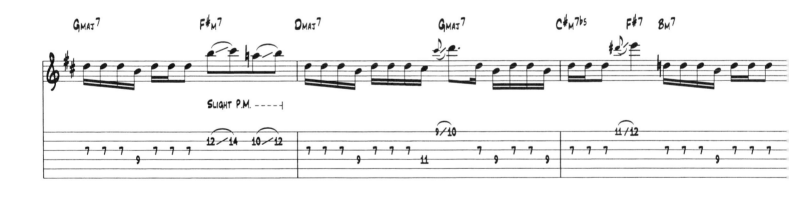
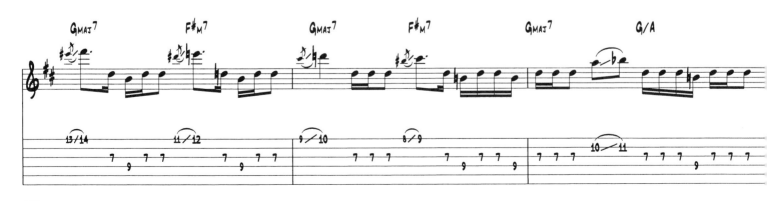

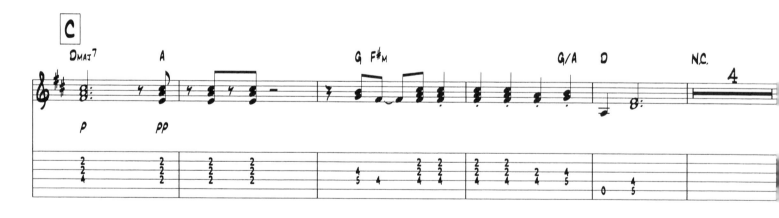
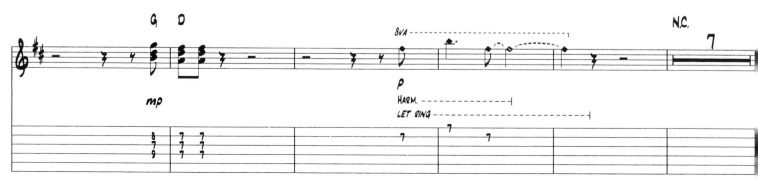

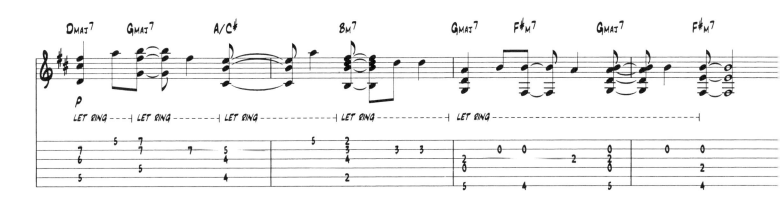
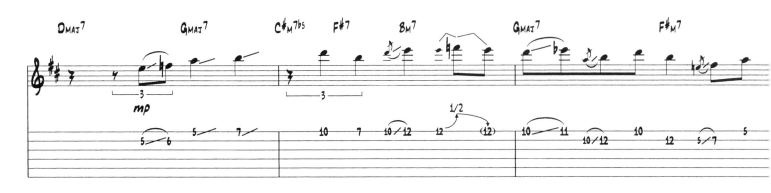

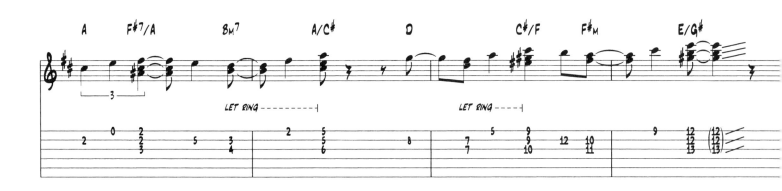
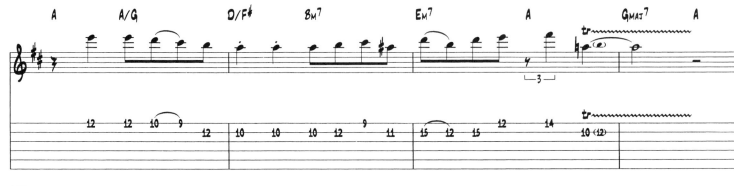

150

Unity Village

By Pat Metheny

*Chord symbols reflect basic harmony.

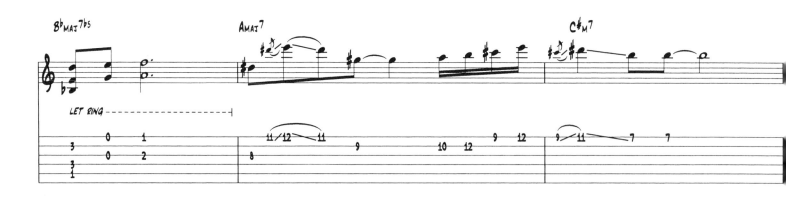

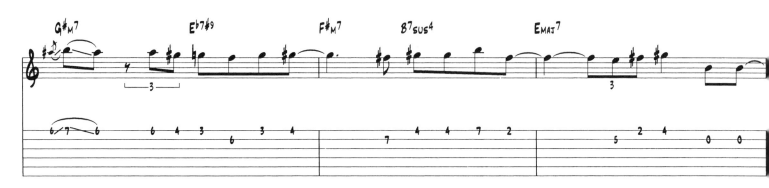

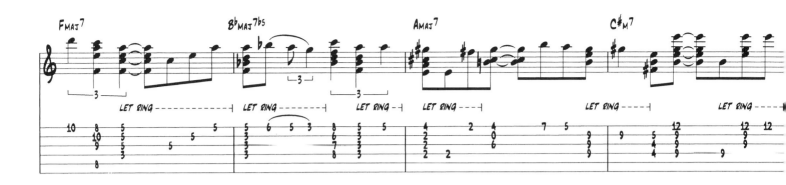

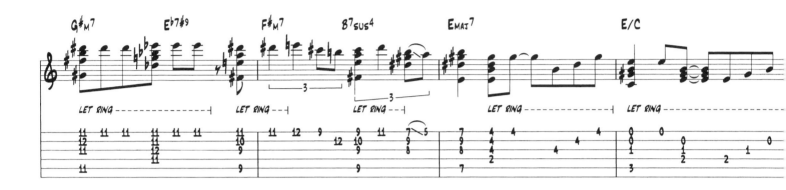

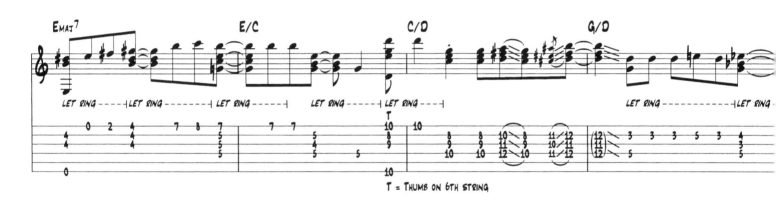

T = Thumb on 6th string

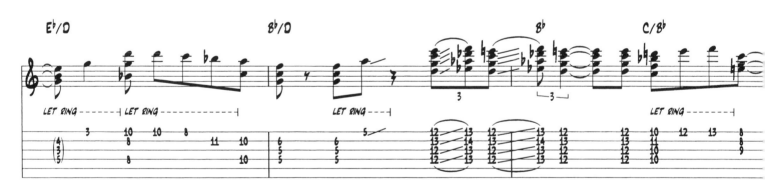

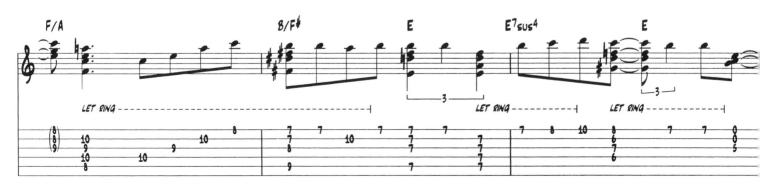

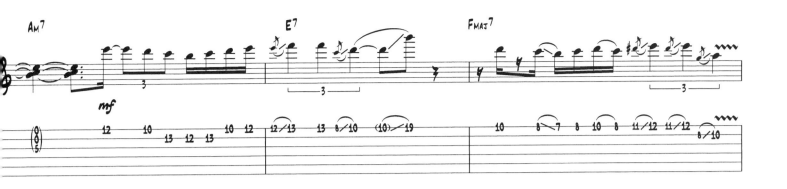

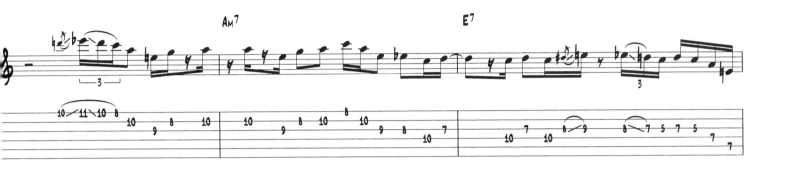

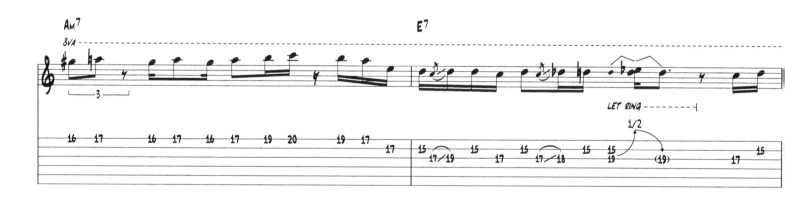

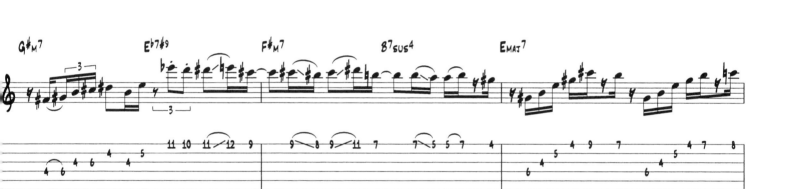

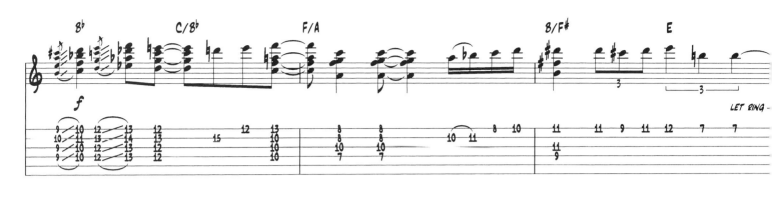

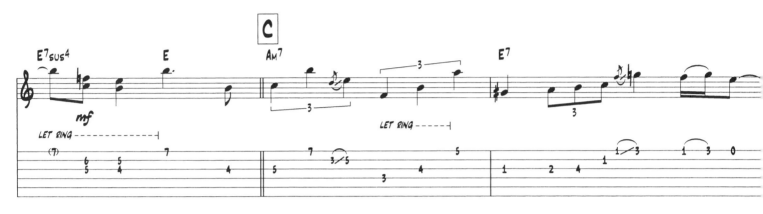

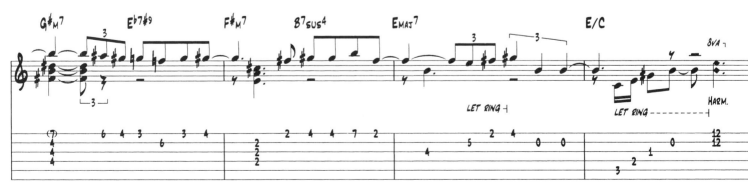

Soul Cowboy

By Pat Metheny

*Chord symbols reflect basic harmony.

**Played as even eighth notes.

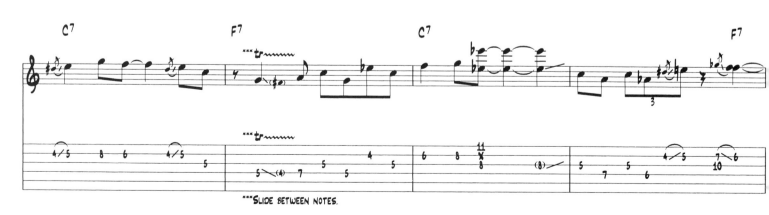

***Slide between notes.

*Played as even eighth notes.

**Played behind the beat.

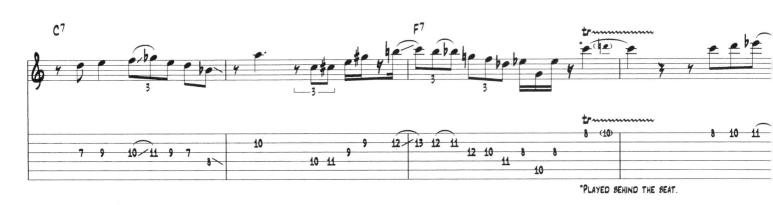

*PLAYED BEHIND THE BEAT.

*Played behind the beat.

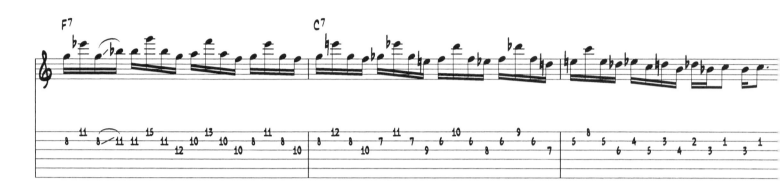

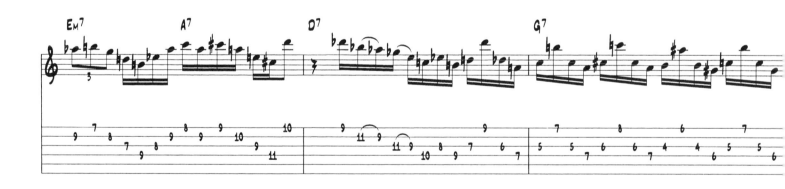

164

165

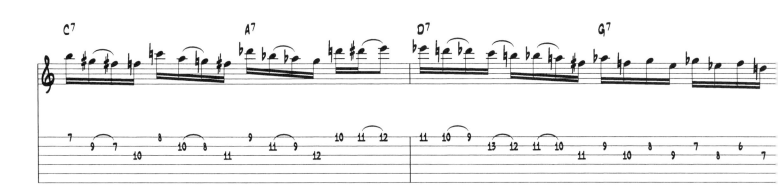

168

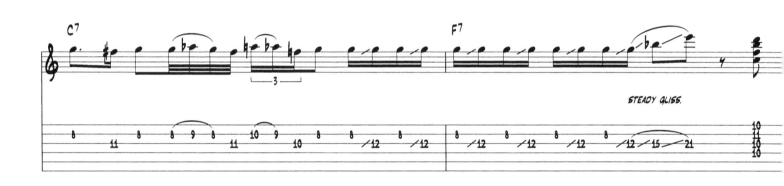

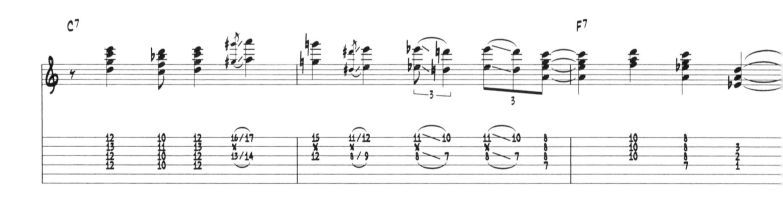

170

*PLAYED BEHIND THE BEAT.

LET RING

STEADY GLISS.

*Played behind the beat.

173

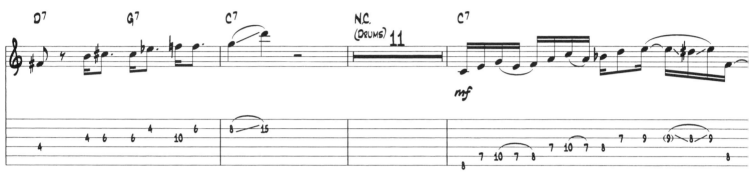

174

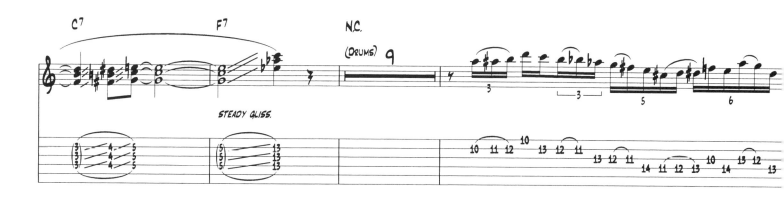

176

*PLAYED BEHIND THE BEAT.

*Played as even eighth notes.

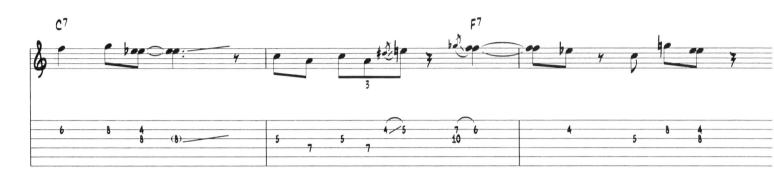

**Played as even eighth notes.

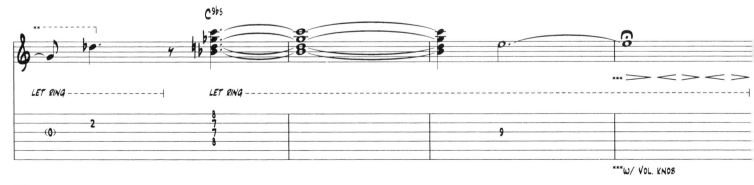

***w/ Vol. Knob

NIGHT TURNS INTO DAY

By Pat Metheny

*Chord symbols reflect implied harmony.

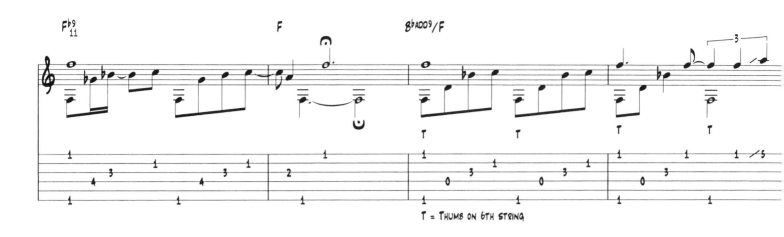

T = THUMB ON 6TH STRING

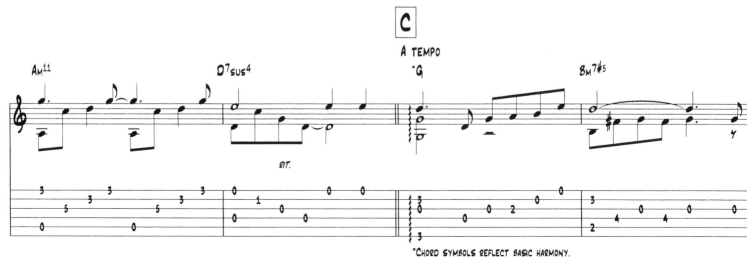

*CHORD SYMBOLS REFLECT BASIC HARMONY.

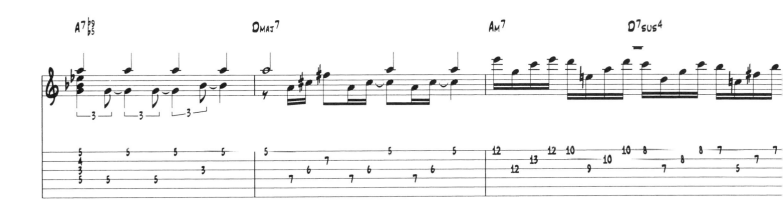

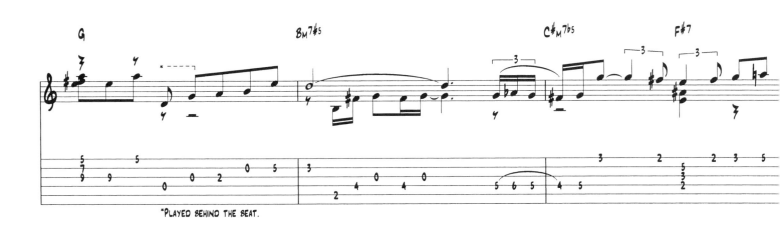

*Played behind the beat.

**Vibrato both notes.

*Played behind the beat.

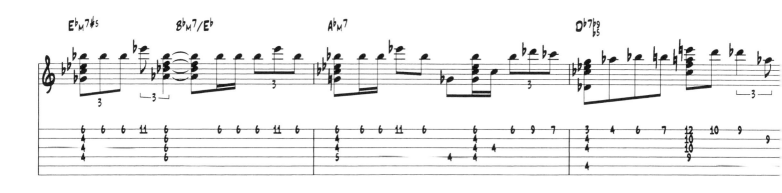

*Pick near bridge (next 9 meas.).   **Played behind the beat.

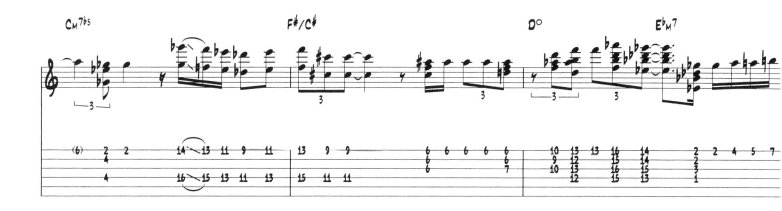

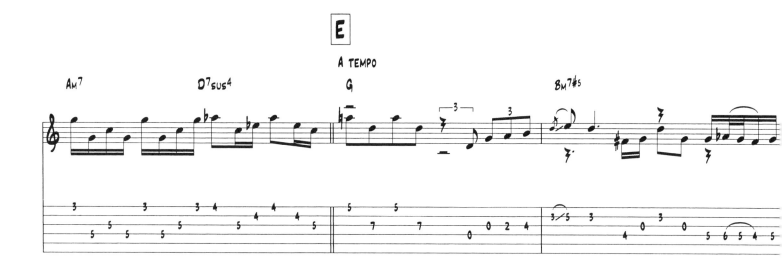

*Played behind the beat.

*VIBRATO BOTH NOTES.

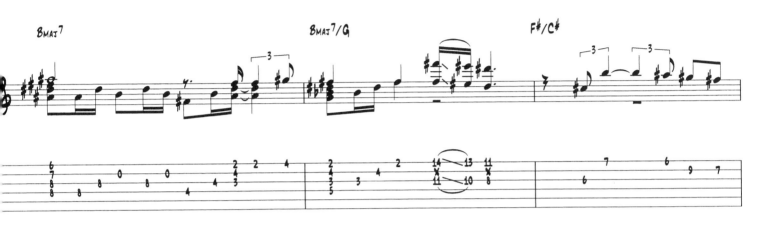

FREE TIME

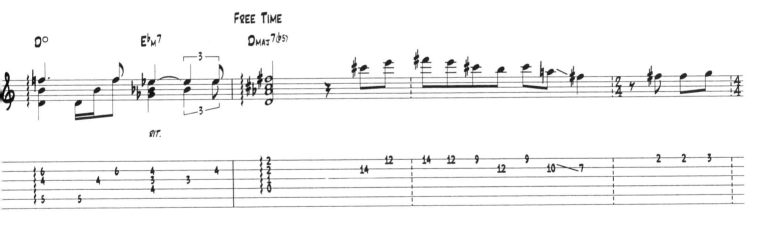

RIT.

**TREMOLO WITH THUMB.

Faith Healer

By Pat Metheny

*w/ overdrive, harmonist & delay

*Boss ME-50 Guitar Multi-Effects.

Set-up: Overdrive = Type MT-2
        Modulation = Type harmonist, adding a minor 3rd above
        Delay = Type analog

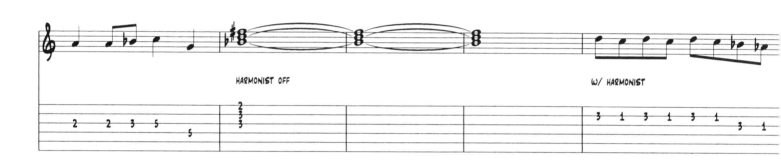

188

*HARMONIST SET-UP: ADD AN OCTAVE BELOW.

**GTR. 1: GUITAR FRENZY

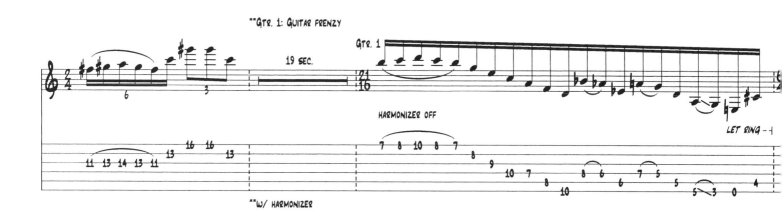

**W/ HARMONIZER

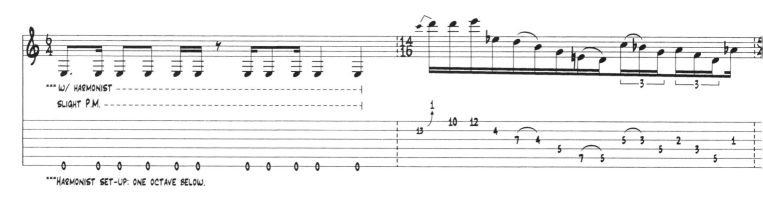

***HARMONIST SET-UP: ONE OCTAVE BELOW.

*Harmonist set-up: add a minor 3rd above.

**Notes recorded with the digital delay "hold" depressed.

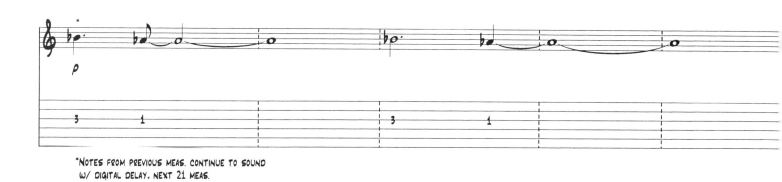

*NOTES FROM PREVIOUS MEAS. CONTINUE TO SOUND
 W/ DIGITAL DELAY. NEXT 21 MEAS.

G

Gtr. 1: w/ random sounds & effects

5:48

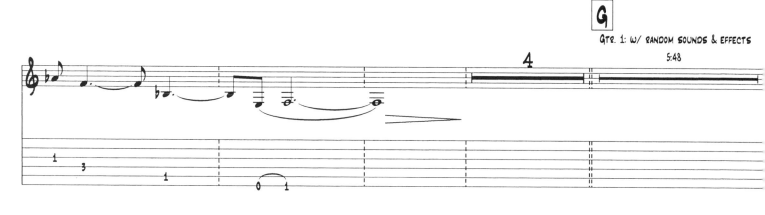

H

(9:38)

Gtr. 1

HARMONIST FRENZY

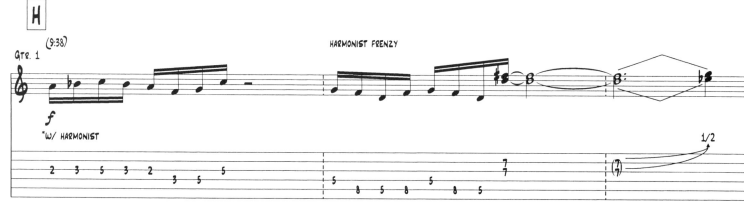

*W/ HARMONIST

*HARMONIST SET-UP: ADD A PERFECT 4TH BELOW.

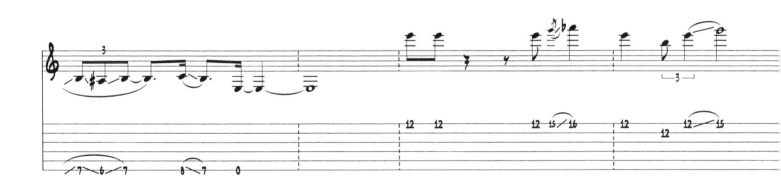

194

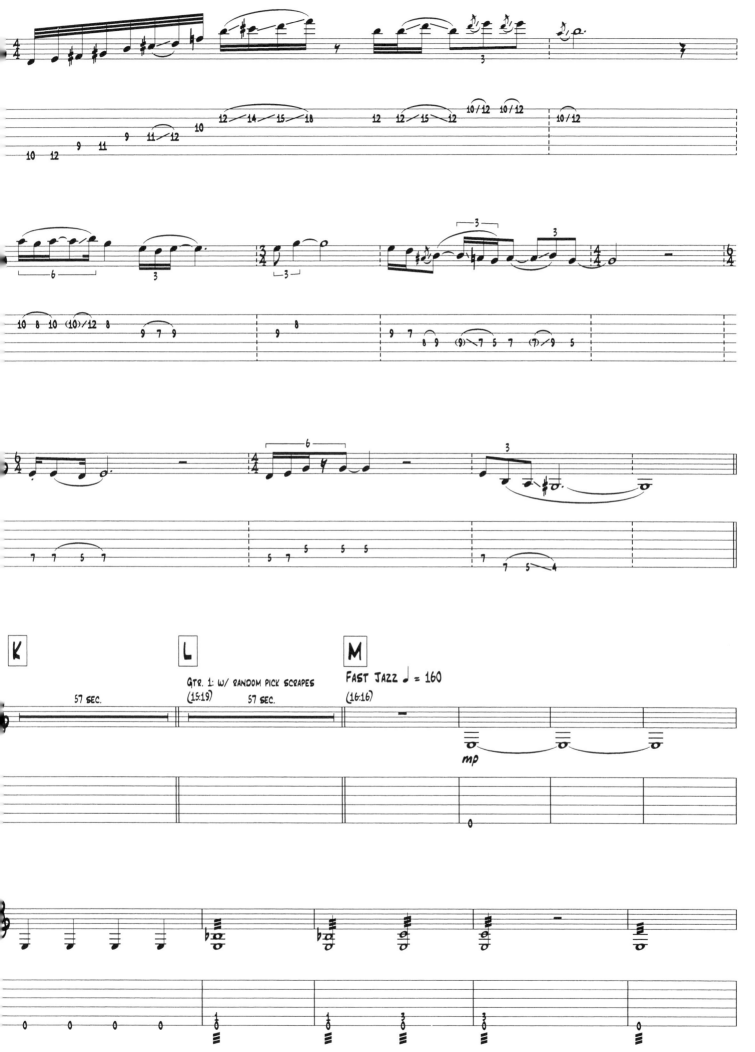

198

Counting Texas

By Pat Metheny

**Chord symbols reflect implied harmony.

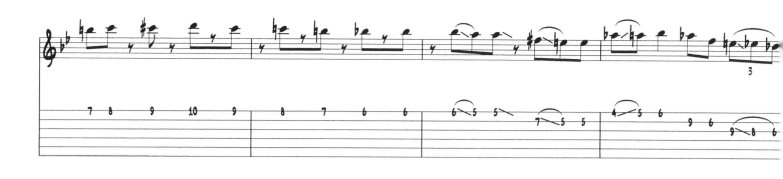

205

206

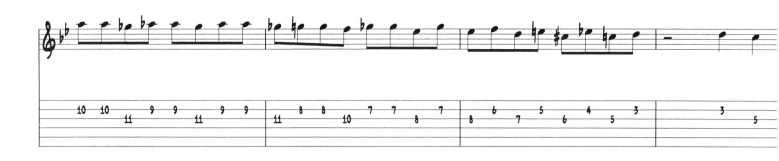
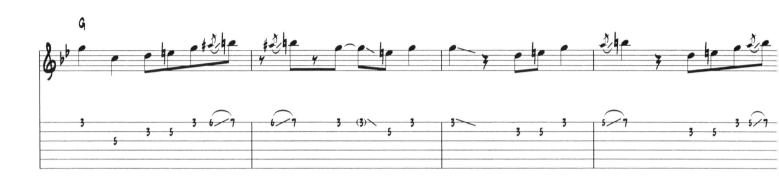

*GTR.: RANDOMLY PICK STRINGS BEHIND THE BRIDGE.

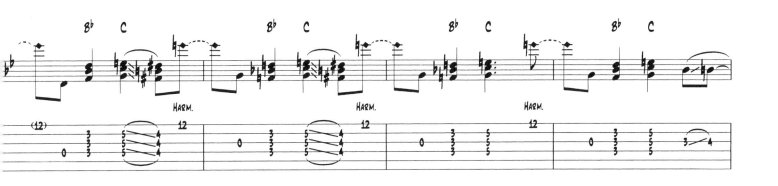

Guitar Notation Legend

Guitar Music can be notated three different ways: on a *musical staff*, in *tablature*, and in *rhythm slashes*.

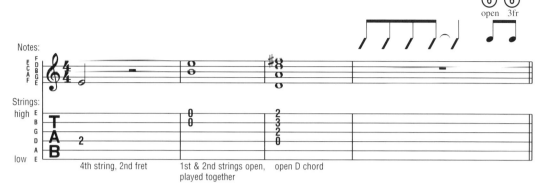

RHYTHM SLASHES are written above the staff. Strum chords in the rhythm indicated. Use the chord diagrams found at the top of the first page of the transcription for the appropriate chord voicings. Round noteheads indicate single notes.

THE MUSICAL STAFF shows pitches and rhythms and is divided by bar lines into measures. Pitches are named after the first seven letters of the alphabet.

TABLATURE graphically represents the guitar fingerboard. Each horizontal line represents a string, and each number represents a fret.

Notes:

Strings:
high
low

4th string, 2nd fret | 1st & 2nd strings open, played together | open D chord

---

HALF-STEP BEND: Strike the note and bend up 1/2 step.

WHOLE-STEP BEND: Strike the note and bend up one step.

GRACE NOTE BEND: Strike the note and immediately bend up as indicated.

SLIGHT (MICROTONE) BEND: Strike the note and bend up 1/4 step.

BEND AND RELEASE: Strike the note and bend up as indicated, then release back to the original note. Only the first note is struck.

PRE-BEND: Bend the note as indicated, then strike it.

VIBRATO: The string is vibrated by rapidly bending and releasing the note with the fretting hand.

WIDE VIBRATO: The pitch is varied to a greater degree by vibrating with the fretting hand.

HAMMER-ON: Strike the first (lower) note with one finger, then sound the higher note (on the same string) with another finger by fretting it without picking.

PULL-OFF: Place both fingers on the notes to be sounded. Strike the first note and without picking, pull the finger off to sound the second (lower) note.

LEGATO SLIDE: Strike the first note and then slide the same fret-hand finger up or down to the second note. The second note is not struck.

SHIFT SLIDE: Same as legato slide, except the second note is struck.

TRILL: Very rapidly alternate between the notes indicated by continuously hammering on and pulling off.

TAPPING: Hammer ("tap") the fret indicated with the pick-hand index or middle finger and pull off to the note fretted by the fret hand.

NATURAL HARMONIC: Strike the note while the fret-hand lightly touches the string directly over the fret indicated.

PINCH HARMONIC: The note is fretted normally and a harmonic is produced by adding the edge of the thumb or the tip of the index finger of the pick hand to the normal pick attack.

PICK SCRAPE: The edge of the pick is rubbed down (or up) the string, producing a scratchy sound.

MUFFLED STRINGS: A percussive sound is produced by laying the fret hand across the string(s) without depressing, and striking them with the pick hand.

PALM MUTING: The note is partially muted by the pick hand lightly touching the string(s) just before the bridge.

RAKE: Drag the pick across the strings indicated with a single motion.

TREMOLO PICKING: The note is picked as rapidly and continuously as possible.

VIBRATO BAR DIVE AND RETURN: The pitch of the note or chord is dropped a specified number of steps (in rhythm) then returned to the original pitch.

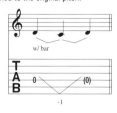

VIBRATO BAR SCOOP: Depress the bar just before striking the note, then quickly release the bar.

VIBRATO BAR DIP: Strike the note and then immediately drop a specified number of steps, then release back to the original pitch.

PLAY THE CLASSICS
JAZZ FOLIOS FOR GUITARISTS

BEST OF JAZZ GUITAR
by Wolf Marshall • Signature Licks

In this book/CD pack, Wolf Marshall provides a hands-on analysis of 10 of the most frequently played tunes in the jazz genre, as played by the leading guitarists of all time. Features: All the Things You Are • How Insensitive • I'll Remember April • So What • Yesterdays • and more.
00695586 Book/CD Pack......................$24.95

50 ESSENTIAL BEBOP HEADS ARRANGED FOR GUITAR

The best lines of Charlie Parker, Dizzy Gillespie, Thelonious Monk, and many more, for guitar with notes and tab. Includes: Donna Lee • Groovin' High • Ornithology • Confirmation • Epistrophy • and more.
00698990 ....$14.95

GUITAR STANDARDS
Classic Jazz Masters Series

16 classic jazz guitar performances transcribed note for note with tablature: All of You (Kenny Burrell) • Easter Parade (Herb Ellis) • I'll Remember April (Grant Green) • Lover Man (Django Reinhardt) • Song for My Father (George Benson) • The Way You Look Tonight (Wes Montgomery) • and more. Includes a discography.
00699143 Guitar Transcriptions $14.95

JAZZ BALLADS FOR FINGERSTYLE GUITAR

21 standards, including: Cry Me a River • Easy to Love • In a Sentimental Mood • Isn't It Romantic? • Mood Indigo • My Funny Valentine • My Romance • Some Enchanted Evening • Stella by Starlight • The Way You Look Tonight • When I Fall in Love • and more.
00699028 Fingerstyle Guitar $12.95

JAZZ CLASSICS FOR SOLO GUITAR
arranged by Robert B. Yelin

This collection includes excellent chord melody arrangements in standard notation and tablature for 35 all-time jazz favorites: April in Paris • Cry Me a River • Day by Day • God Bless' the Child • It Might as Well Be Spring • Lover • My Romance • Nuages • Satin Doll • Tenderly • Unchained Melody • Wave • and more!
00699279 Solo Guitar $17.95

JAZZ FAVORITES FOR SOLO GUITAR
arranged by Robert B. Yelin

This fantastic 35-song collection includes lush chord melody arrangements in standard notation and tab: Autumn in New York • Call Me Irresponsible • How Deep Is the Ocean • I Could Write a Book • The Lady Is a Tramp • Mood Indigo • Polka Dots and Moonbeams • Solitude • Take the "A" Train • Where or When • more.
00699278 Solo Guitar $17.95

JAZZ GEMS FOR SOLO GUITAR
arranged by Robert B. Yelin

35 great solo arrangements of jazz classics, including: After You've Gone • Alice in Wonderland • The Christmas Song • Four • Meditation • Stompin' at the Savoy • Sweet and Lovely • Waltz for Debby • Yardbird Suite • You'll Never Walk Alone • You've Changed • and more.
00699617 Solo Guitar $17.95

JAZZ GUITAR BIBLE

The one book that has all of the jazz guitar classics transcribed note-for-note, with standard notation and tablature. Includes over 30 songs: Body and Soul • Girl Talk • I'll Remember April • In a Sentimental Mood • My Funny Valentine • Nuages • Satin Doll • So What • Stardust • Take Five • Tangerine • Yardbird Suite • and more.
00690466 Guitar Recorded Versions $19.95

JAZZ GUITAR CHORD MELODIES
arranged & performed by Dan Towey

This book/CD pack includes complete solo performances of 12 standards, including: All the Things You Are • Body and Soul • My Romance • How Insensitive • My One and Only Love • and more. The arrangements are performance level and range in difficulty from intermediate to advanced.
00698988 Book/CD Pack $19.95

JAZZ GUITAR PLAY-ALONG
Guitar Play-Along Volume 16

With this book/CD pack, all you have to do is follow the tab, listen to the CD to hear how the guitar should sound, and then play along using the separate backing tracks. 8 songs: All Blues • Bluesette • Footprints • How Insensitive (Insensatez) • Misty • Satin Doll • Stella by Starlight • Tenor Madness.
00699584 Book/CD Pack $12.95

THE JAZZ STANDARDS BOOK

106 fantastic standards in easy guitar format (without tablature). Songs include: Ain't Misbehavin' • Blue Skies • Come Rain or Come Shine • Fly Me to the Moon • Georgia on My Mind • How High the Moon • It Don't Mean a Thing (If It Ain't Got That Swing) • My Romance • Slightly Out of Tune • Tangerine • and more.
00702164 Easy Guitar $15.95

JAZZ STANDARDS FOR FINGERSTYLE GUITAR

20 songs, including: All the Things You Are • Autumn Leaves • Bluesette • Body and Soul • Fly Me to the Moon • The Girl from Ipanema • How Insensitive • I've Grown Accustomed to Her Face • My Funny Valentine • Satin Doll • Stompin' at the Savoy • and more.
00699029 Fingerstyle Guitar $10.95

JAZZ STANDARDS FOR SOLO GUITAR
arranged by Robert B. Yelin

35 chord melody guitar arrangements, including: Ain't Misbehavin' • Autumn Leaves • Bewitched • Cherokee • Darn That Dream • Girl Talk • I've Got You Under My Skin • Lullaby of Birdland • My Funny Valentine • A Nightingale Sang in Berkeley Square • Stella by Starlight • The Very Thought of You • and more.
00699277 Solo Guitar $17.95

FOR MORE INFORMATION, SEE YOUR LOCAL MUSIC DEALER, OR WRITE TO:

HAL•LEONARD®
CORPORATION
7777 W. BLUEMOUND RD. P.O. BOX 13819 MILWAUKEE, WI 53213

Visit Hal Leonard Online at **www.halleonard.com**

Prices, contents and availability subject to change without notice.

0805